DAY SKIPPER PRACTICAL COURSE NOTES

This booklet is aimed at illustrating and clarifying the ***PRACTICAL DAY SKIPPER COURSES*** run by RYA recognised sailing schools. It should be used in conjunction with:

- ***Competent Crew Practical Course Notes*** and practical course which cover all aspects of life afloat for those new to the sport.
- ***Day Skipper Shorebased Course Notes*** which covers the theoretical side of navigation and supports the ***Day Skipper Shorebased Courses*** which are run by RYA recognised shorebased schools all over the country.

THE PRACTICAL COURSE

Before attending a Day Skipper practical course you should look at the suggested pre-course experience outlined in the RYA cruising logbook G15. You will need basic navigational knowledge and sailing ability.

- Navigational knowledge is best obtained by attending an RYA ***Day Skipper Shorebased Course.***
- Basic sailing ability can be defined as being able to sail reasonably efficiently around a triangular course, being able to tack, gybe, sail on all points of sailing and control boat speed. An RYA ***Level 2 Dinghy Sailing Course*** gives an ideal introduction to the beginner.

Discuss your level of ability with the sailing school to ensure that you are taught to the right level and gain maximum benefit from the course.

TAKING COMMAND

During the Day Skipper course you will be shown the pleasures and pitfalls of taking command. You will be taught how to take charge of the yacht for a short passage. This will involve planning the trip, briefing the crew, boat handling, navigation and many of the other skills described in these course notes. The instructor will encourage you to take responsibility for your decisions and illustrate that, in return for taking the credit when things go well, the skipper must also take responsibility and make decisions when things go wrong. At the end of the course you should understand your strengths and weaknesses and have learnt how to undertake safe, relaxed passages as skipper within a limited area.

Your instructor will understand that you and the other course members are new to skippering and will make sure that the yacht does not stand into danger. Finally remember that the reason for becoming more proficient is to gain more pleasure from the sport.

SAFETY

As skipper, you shouldn't take a boat away from the dock without checking all the safety equipment. Also *everyone* on board should know where it is and how to use it. (*See RYA booklet C8.*)
This is easier said than done as everyone is keen to get away and go sailing, BUT as skipper it is your responsibility to check...

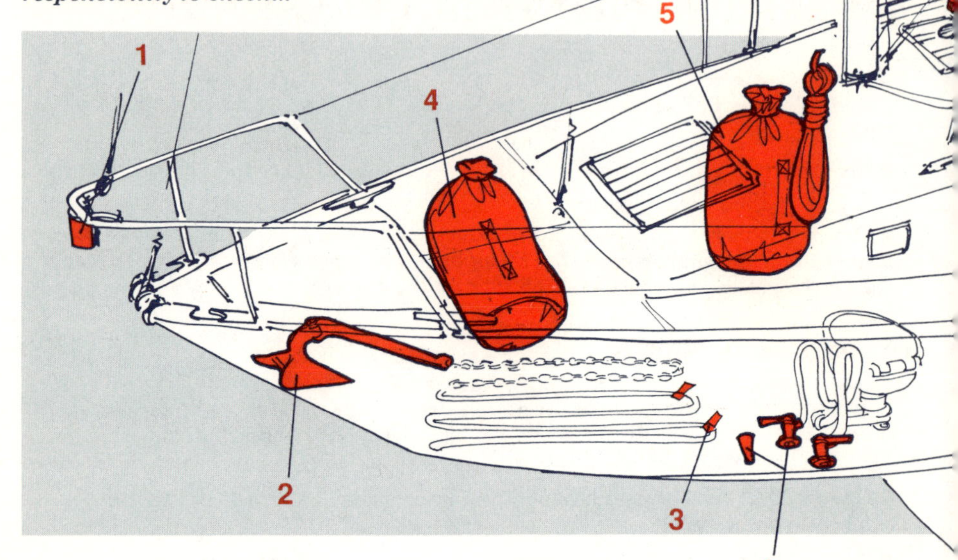

1. Do the navigation lights work - are there spare bulbs ?
2. Are there adequate anchors on board - are they stowed safely ?
3. Is the anchor cable in good condition, well secured and how are the depths marked ?
4. Is there a dinghy on board with oars, repair kit, pump and anchor ?
5. Are there enough sails, warps and at least two winch handles?
   It's worth checking them over and stowing them neatly as this gives you more space.
6. Do the sea cocks work? Are there wooden bungs to seal them off in case of accident ?
7. Have you got enough navigation equipment - charts, pilots, tide-tables etc ?
8. Is the first aid kit adequate ? (*See RYA booklet G6.*)
9. Do the tools work ? (Or are they a heap of rust ?)
10. Are the flares O.K. ? (Check dates.)
11. Does the engine work ? Is there a handbook, starting handle, spares etc? (*See page 5*)
12. Have you enough fuel and water ?
13. Is there enough gas and is the installation safe ?

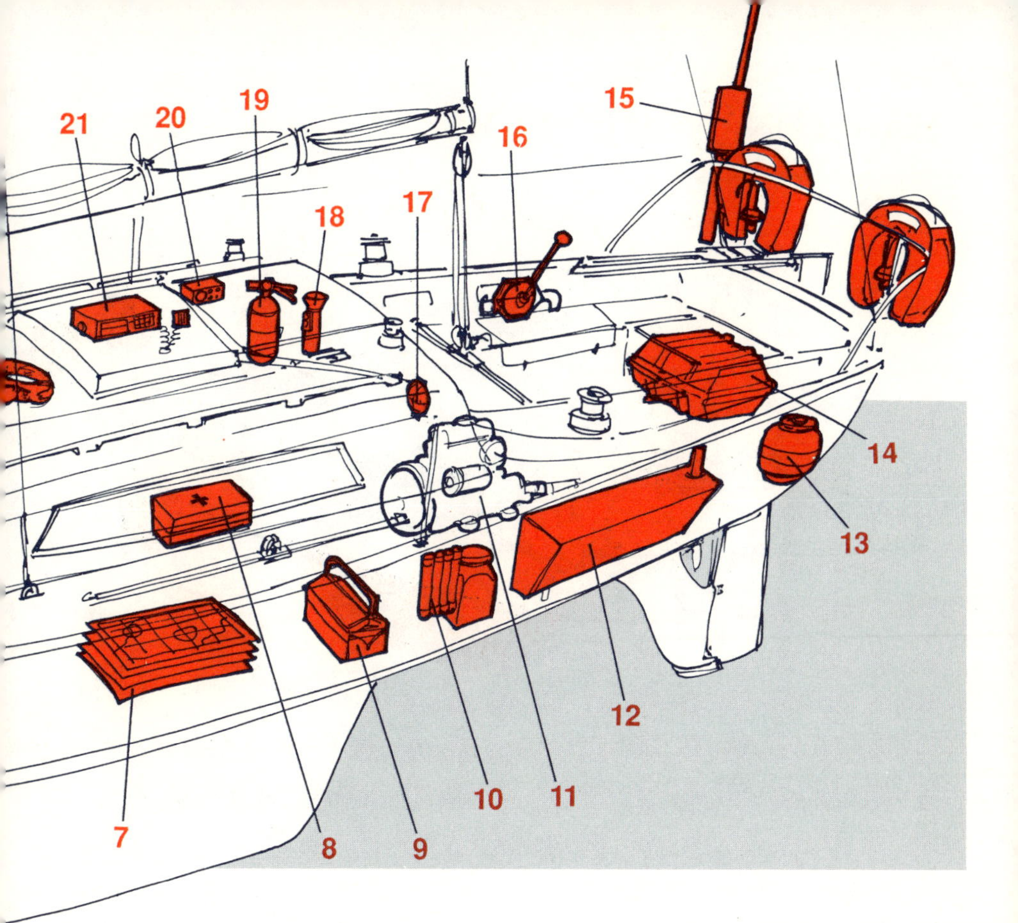

14. Check the life-raft service log.

15. Can the *'man-overboard'* gear be released quickly ?
Do the lights work and are there spare batteries and bulbs ?

16. Do the bilge pumps work, can you clear them, is there a *'strum-box'*,
could you change the diaphragm and is there a strong bucket too ?

17. Are the main and hand bearing compasses accurate ? Is there a deviation card ?

18. Do the torches have spare batteries and bulbs ?

19. Have the fire-extinguishers been well maintained ? Are there enough ?

20. Does the echo-sounder work ? Is there a lead line ?

21. Can *everyone* on board make a radio distress call and activate the EPIRB (if carried) ?
Do you understand the limitations of all the other electrical nav. equipment on board ?

22 Does each crew member have a safety harness and lifejacket ?
Are they in good condition ?

CHECK: GAS, SMOKE AND WATER WARNING DEVICES, IF FITTED

MAINTENANCE CHECKS

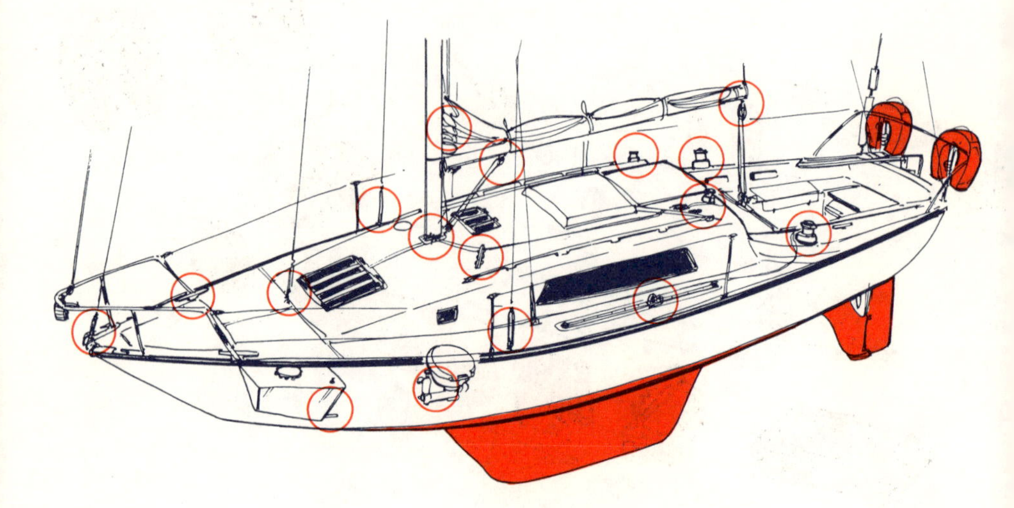

As skipper you are responsible for all maintenance from the aerial at the masthead to the paint under the keel. This daunting task has been somewhat lessened today by the introduction of modern materials, which need less love and care, **BUT** they still need some!

STANDING RIGGING: Check for broken strands, cracks in end fittings, loose pins, wear in joints. Tape over ends of pins etc. but also check under old tape.

RUNNING RIGGING: Check for chafe, frayed end fittings, replace worn whippings etc.

SPARS: Check for dents, loose fittings, cracks and chafe.

ALL THE ABOVE WILL NEED A PERIODIC TRIP TO THE MASTHEAD.

SAILS: Check stitching and fittings.

HULL AND DECK: Check for signs of strain (small cracks) around mast and other deck fittings. Check windows and hatches for leaks. Keep paint and varnish work in good order. Make sure non-slip deck isn't worn. Keep bottom clean.

WINCHES AND BLOCKS: Check for wear and tear, keep well lubricated, service regularly.

PIPES AND TANKS: Check all joints, keep clean, look for signs of chafe (take great care of fuel pipes, gas lines and sea cocks).

ELECTRICITY: Check batteries are well secured, joints well made, wiring adequate and that battery charging won't cause interference to navigational instruments.

BILGES: Check for leaks and keep them clean.

KEEP A MAINTENANCE LOG
AND GET ALL THE CREW TO REPORT ANY PROBLEMS THEY SEE.

MARINE DIESEL ENGINES

Always read the handbook.

KEEP A CHECK ON:

- fuel and oil levels,
- stern gland (greaser),
- battery charging,
- engine temperature and oil pressure.

ALWAYS CHECK THAT COOLING WATER IS COMING OUT OF THE EXHAUST PIPE.

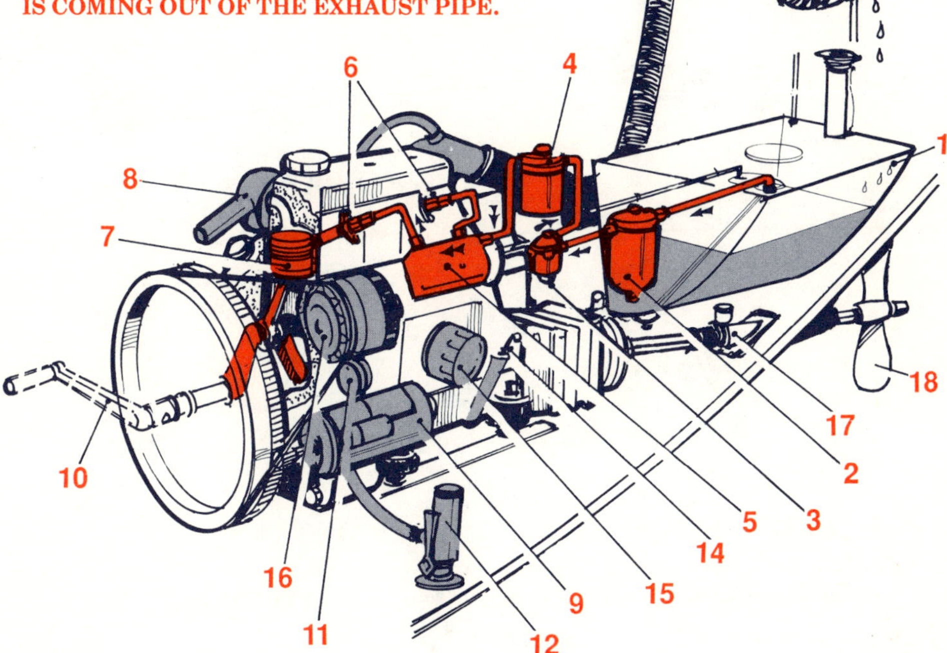

Marine diesels need clean fuel, free from ***dirt, water and air.***
Any one of these will stop it dead!
The fuel tanks should be kept as full as possible because this will prevent condensation forming in the **air above the fuel (1)**. The **primary filter (2)** extracts most of the moisture and dirt, while the **fuel pump (3)** drives the fuel through an even finer **secondary filter (4)**. The **injection pump (5)** measures out the clean fuel and delivers it to the cylinder via the **injectors (6)**. The **piston (7)** compresses the fuel and air (which comes in via the **air filter (8)** until the gas gets so hot that it explodes, driving the piston down again. The whole process is started by turning the engine over with the **starter motor (9)** or by cranking the **handle (10)**. A **water pump (11)** cools the engine by sucking in the water through a **sea cock / filter (12)** and pumping it around until it comes out through the **exhaust pipe (13)**. Check the oil level with the **dipstick (14)** and change the **oil filter (15)** regularly. Electricity is generated by a belt rotating the **alternator (16)**. The propeller shaft passes through a **stern gland (17)** to the **propeller (18)**.

PASSAGE PLANNING

Green River towards *Red River.*

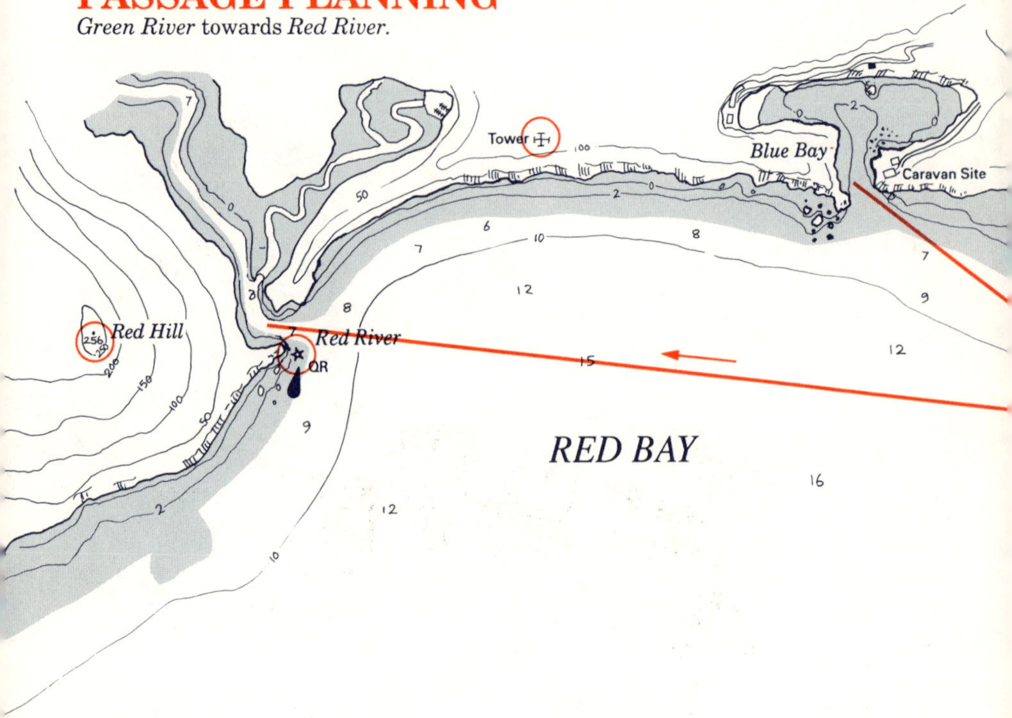

- Look at the entire passage on a small scale chart.
  Check time and distances involved.
- Identify the best route.
  You could go direct to *Red River* but maybe you could stop for lunch at *Blue Bay* ?
- What's the weather forecast ? (*see page 8*)
- What's the tide doing ? (*see page 9*)
- Check large scale charts and pilotage information: departure port, arrival port and diversion ports (*Green River, Red River, Blue Bay* and *Black Bay*).
  Ask others who have been there recently as pilot books can get out of date very quickly.
- Note any hazards on route.
  Green Shoal, Blue Shoal and rocks off *Blue Bay*
- What navigation aids are there?
  Buoys marking *Green Shoal* and *Blue Shoal*.
  Several conspicuous land marks on high ground on the mainland.
  High offshore islands should be in sight in good visibility.
  Highlight on *Large Rock*.
  Good contour lines to follow in *Red Bay* if it gets foggy.
  Red Hill very high, marking *Red River*.
  Red light at *Red River* entrance.

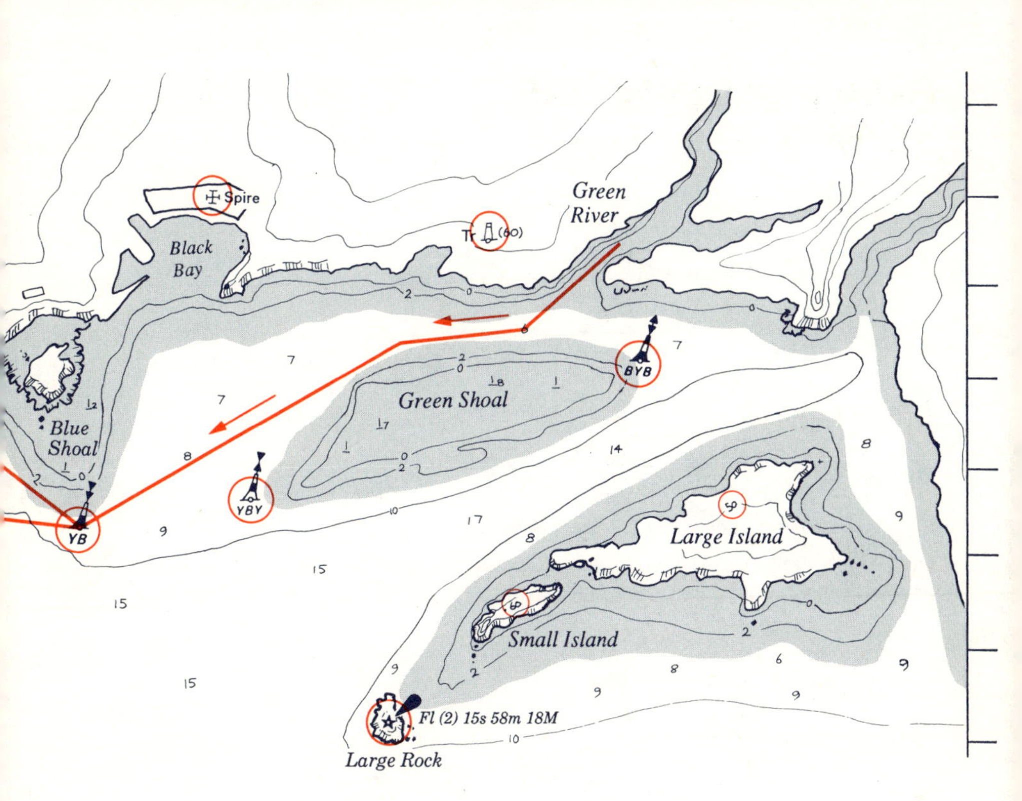

- Correct Charts
- Victual the boat

- Be aware of ...

... military practice areas on the route that might require special attention.

... potential fishing grounds (*shoal areas*) and their attendant hazards (*such as pot buoys etc.*)

... ferry routes particularly those of fast hydrofoils or hovercraft which can appear very quickly and often use the same narrow channels as yachtsmen.

... areas where large ships might be manoeuvring and special regulations might apply.

... the latest local '*Notice to Mariners*' for the area which lists other potential hazards (*such as drilling rigs and pipe laying etc*).

... local events, like regattas and races which will often make popular harbours very crowded.

... seemingly trivial domestic matters such as proximity of fuel and water supplies, banking and shopping facilities (1/2 day closing) and seasonally opening pubs and restaurants.

PASSAGE PLANNING

WEATHER

Draw a rough sketch map of the low's movement if it helps to understand the wind shift.

SHIPPING FORECAST

......Low Tyne 1006 expected Belgium by 1400 Monday.....
Sea areas Portland, Plymouth North West 3 to 4 veering to North later

SO you've got a good wind for the passage

BUT if it had been *North backing West soon* (as below) the last bit of the passage would have meant an unpleasant beat to windward. So maybe you could have gone to *Black Bay* for the day and back in the evening.

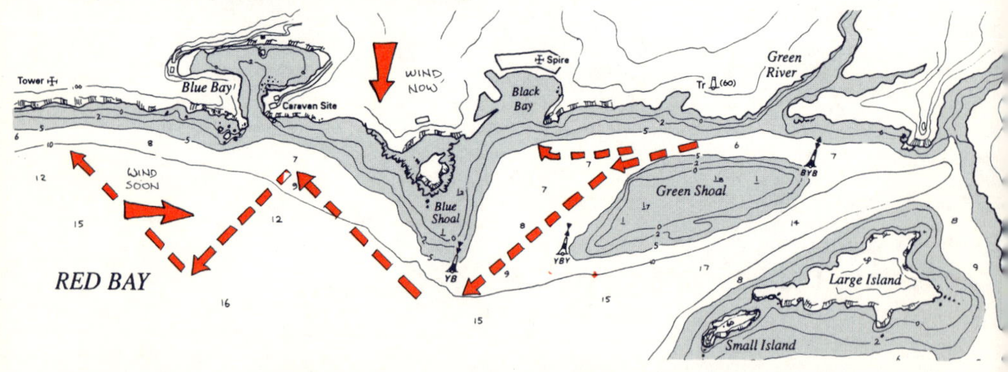

You should try to organise the passage so that you have a favourable tidal stream, particularly around headlands where the flow is strong. The fastest trips are when the wind and tide are both in your favour (BUT bear in mind the return journey!).
If the wind is against you, a fair tide will be very helpful but the sea could be rougher.

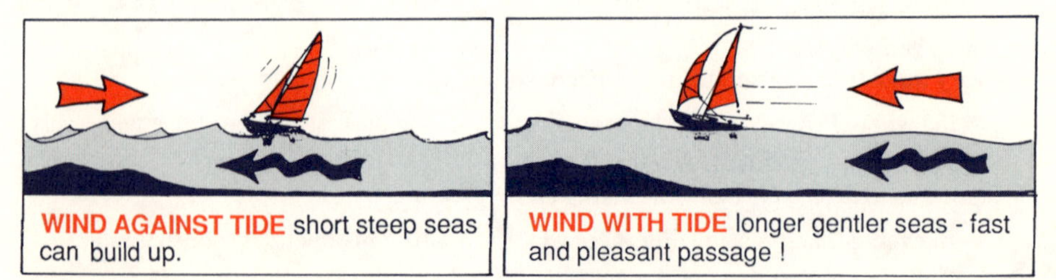

WIND AGAINST TIDE short steep seas can build up.

WIND WITH TIDE longer gentler seas - fast and pleasant passage !

REMEMBER - You have no choice about the wind but you can choose the tide by deciding when to depart. If the wind is unfavourable you could choose another destination.

TIDES

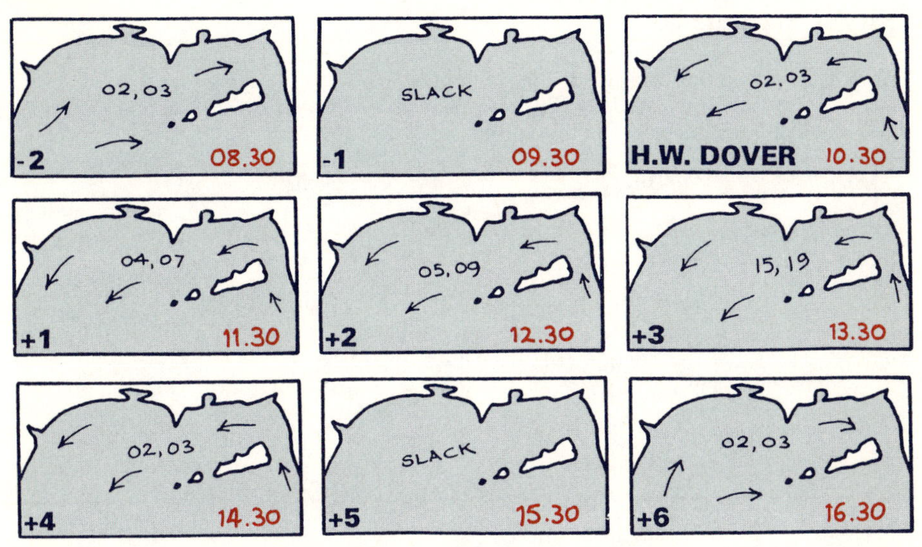

Write in the approximate corrected times on each page of the tidal atlas, (see tide table below).

When is the tide going with you ?

Check to see when there is a favourable West going tide...
It is slack 1 hour before HW then turns West for 5 hours.

What time is HW DOVER ? Is it springs or neaps ?

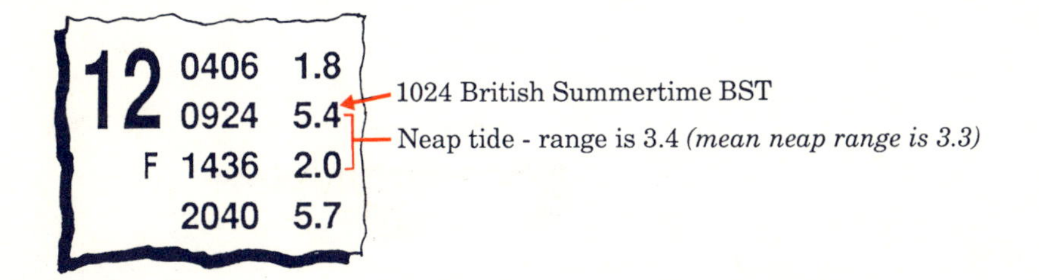

12	0406	1.8
	0924	5.4
F	1436	2.0
	2040	5.7

So with a favourable wind of *North West veering North Force 3 - 4* you could leave around 0930 and cover the 20 odd miles from *Green River* to *Red River* in about 4 hours if you're doing about 5 knots and you'll have a fair tide of about 1/2 knot all the way.

BUT could you stop at *Blue Bay* for lunch ? Is there enough water ?

PASSAGE PLANNING
TIDAL HEIGHTS

Work out the heights of tide for the ports you are likely to visit at the times you are likely to need. (The ***Day Skipper Shorebased Course Notes*** explain how to work out tidal heights from the tide tables.

Green River		*Blue Bay*			*Red River*		
0830	4.1m						
0930	4.2m						
1030	4.3m	1030	4.2m				
		1130	4.3m	(HW)			
		1230	4.2m				
		1330	3.8m	(Range 2.1m)			
		1430	3.2m		1400	3.2m	
		1530	2.6m		1500	2.6m	
					1600	2.2m	
					1700	2.0m	(LW)
					1800	2.2m	
					1900	2.6m	(Range 2.1m)

You could anchor for lunch at *Blue Bay*.

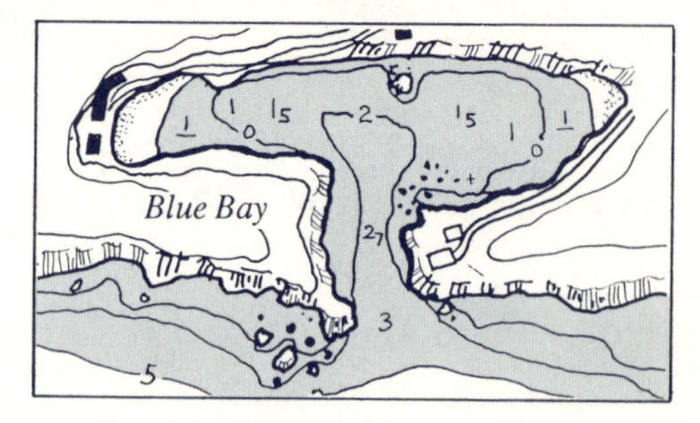

If you arrive at High Water
the most the tide will drop is 2.1m.

To be safe until Low Water you need

	2.1m	(fall of tide = range)
+	1.0m	(draught of yacht)
+	0.5m	(safety margin)
	3.6m of water at 1100	

In fact you will probably arrive after High Water so the tide will fall a little less than the total range.

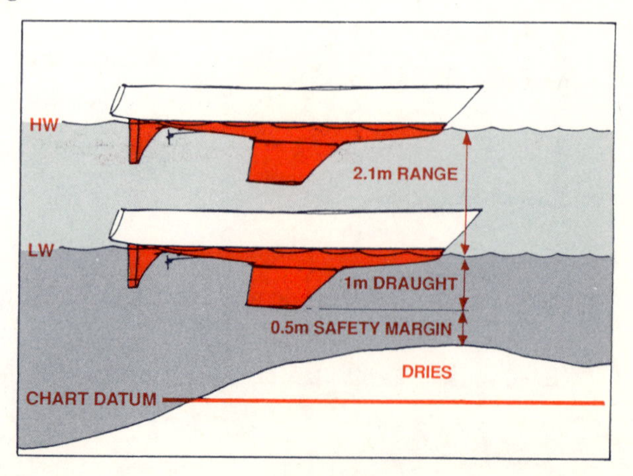

HAZARDS ON ROUTE

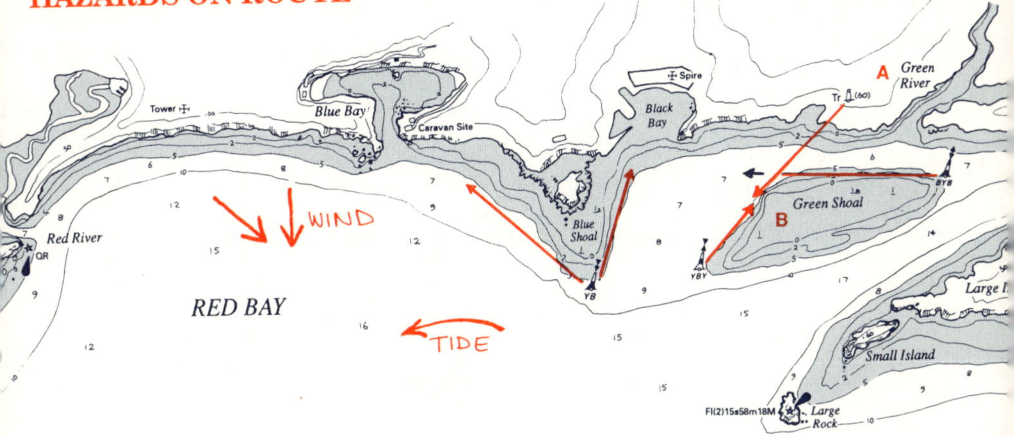

You must shape a course towards the *Blue Shoal* south cardinal buoy.

CLEARING LINES are drawn from the West and East *Green Shoal* cardinal buoys and on both sides of *Blue Shoal* from the south cardinal buoy.
The tower (A) will also give you a line to clear the shoal area at (B)

CLEARING LINES

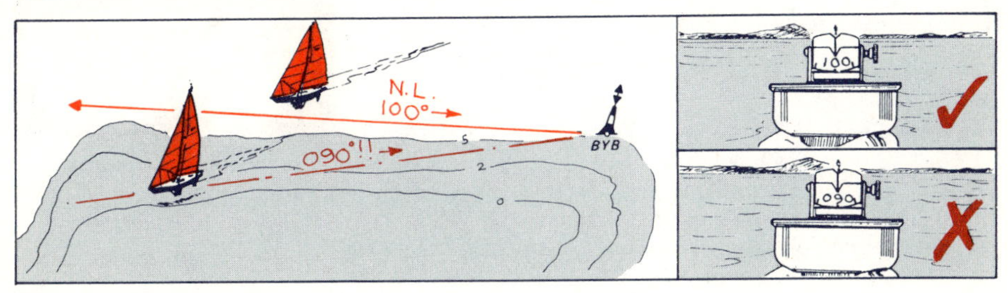

The clearing back bearing on the East cardinal buoy must not be less than 100°. (NL 100° means **<u>N</u>ot <u>L</u>ess** than 100°.)
The shoal area (B) can be missed by sailing on the clearing line until it's crossed by a clearing bearing from the West cardinal or the tower (A).

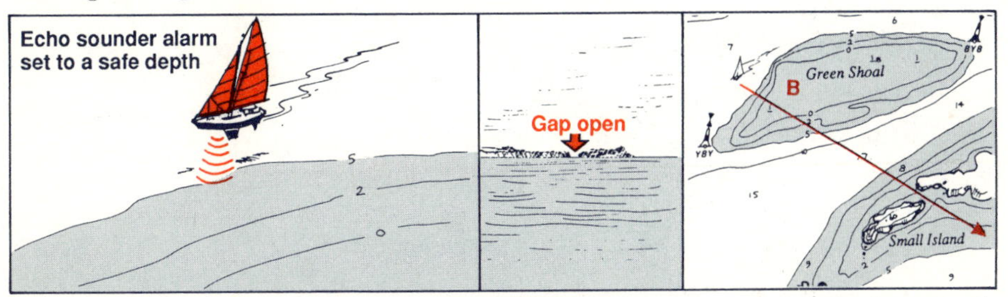

The echo sounder alarm can be set to make sure you don't stray over the shoal area and when the gap between *Small* and *Large Island* opens you've passed the danger (B).

PASSAGE PLANNING

Green River to *Blue Bay*

Blue Bay
Caravan Site
Black Bay
Blue Shoal
YB

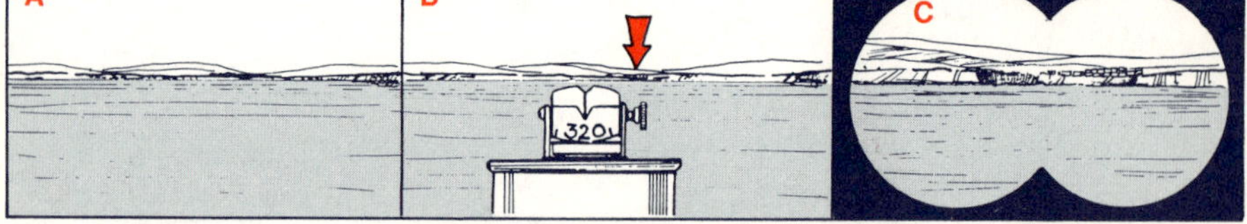

A. *Blue Bay* can be hard to identify, so check what it should bear when you are at the buoy off *Blue Shoal*. At that point you know your exact position - make sure you're ready with the hand bearing compass.
B. Set the hand bearing compass to that bearing and look along it.
C. Check it with the binoculars.

With a *North West or North wind* you will have to beat in so set up clearing lines to define a safe tacking area. The rocks near the entrance to *Blue Bay* could be a hazard. Luckily the entrance to the bay gives you a safe clearing line.

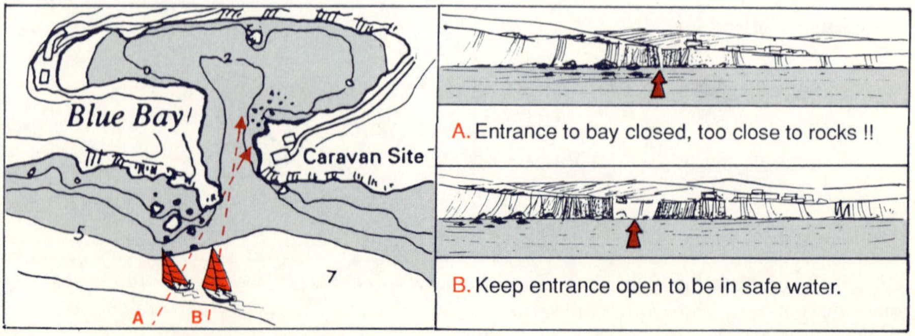

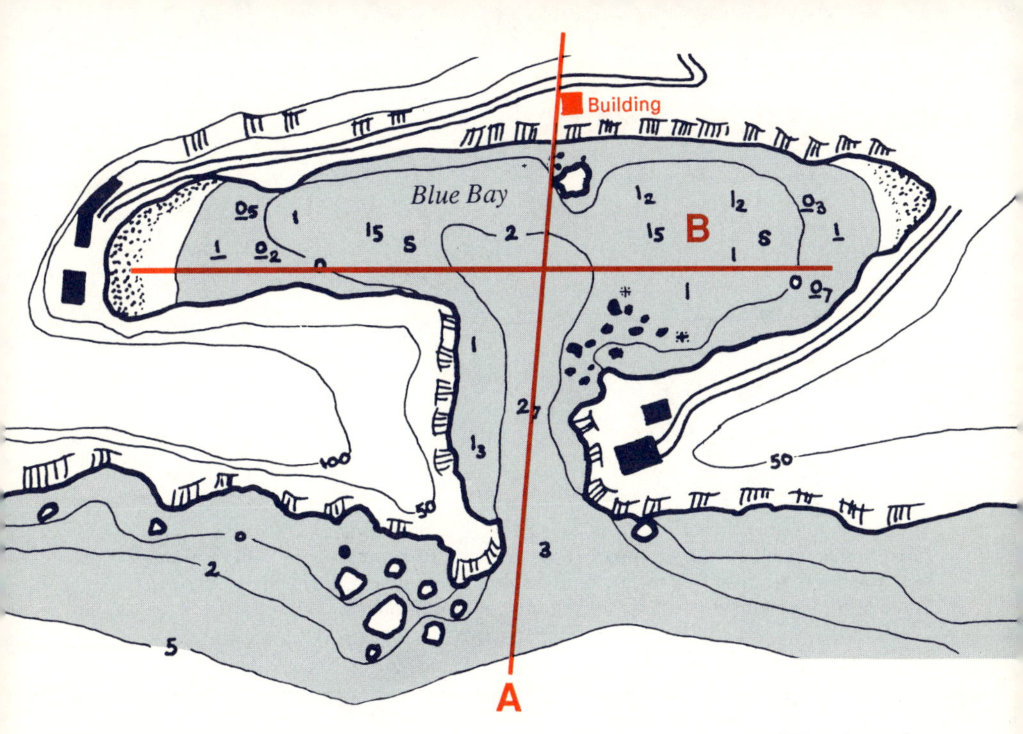

A. When the left hand edges of the house and the rock are in transit you'll be clear of the rocks to starboard.

B. The gap in the buildings shows you when you are past the rocks.
If the anchorage to port is too crowded you can go to the starboard one.

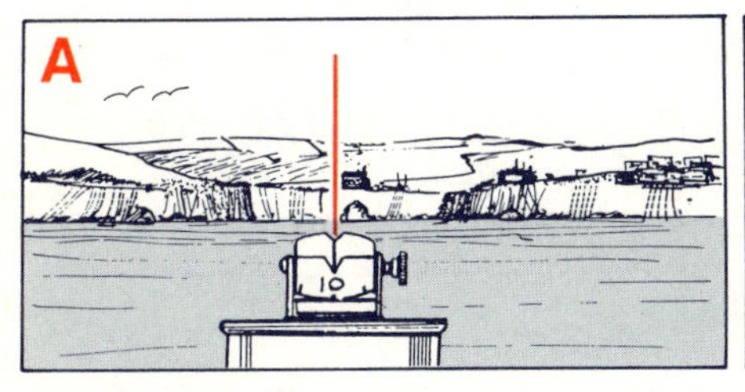

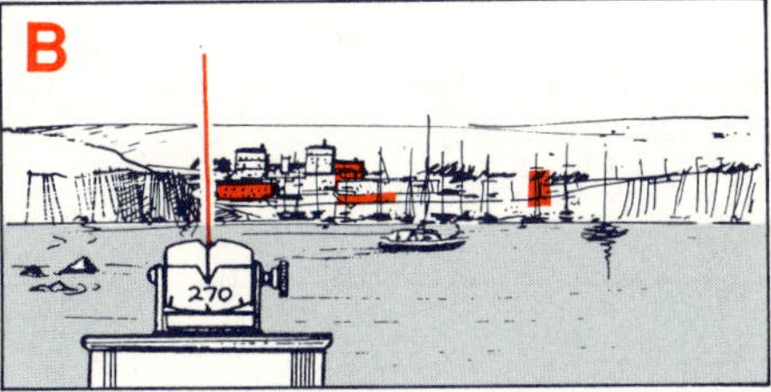

A. Check with compass to see if it's the right transit. (There are often new houses near different rocks !)

B. New buildings *not on chart* but the edge of the bay still gives you a good clearing line to miss the rocks.

You will need to leave *Blue Bay* around 1430 to cover the 8 miles to *Red Bay* with a fair tidal stream. The pilotage into *Red River* is easier after 1700 when the tide is *flooding*.

PASSAGE PLANNING

Blue Bay to Red River

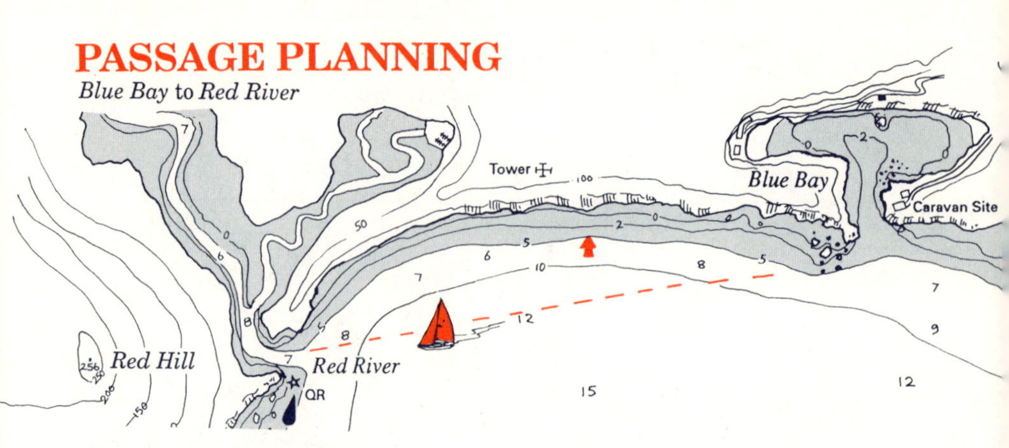

Shape a course towards *Red River* (*see Day Skipper Shorebased Course Notes*).
In this case with a *North or North West* wind it's just a matter of sailing along the coastline and there's a handy 5 metre contour line to follow if the visibility decreases.
You can judge your progress by noting passing land marks.

WHERE'S RED RIVER ?

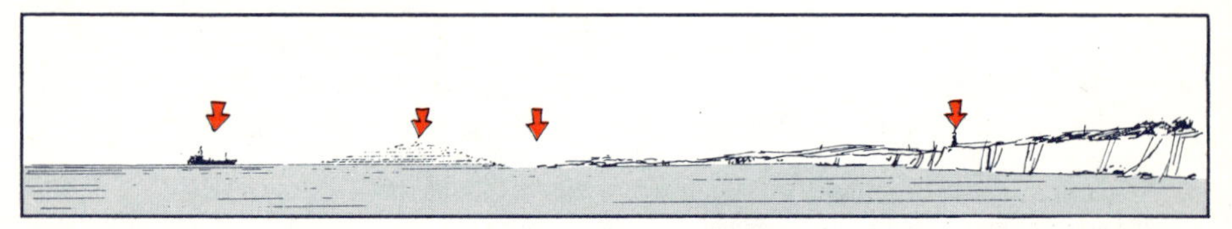

You won't be able to see *Red River* at 8 miles but you might be able to see the high land behind it. Also as you get closer there might be some shipping to point the way (but don't rely on it !).
Red River is a deep water port so make sure you've made note of any harbour regulations that might apply.
Give the marina a call on VHF (channel 80) to see if there's a berth available for the night.

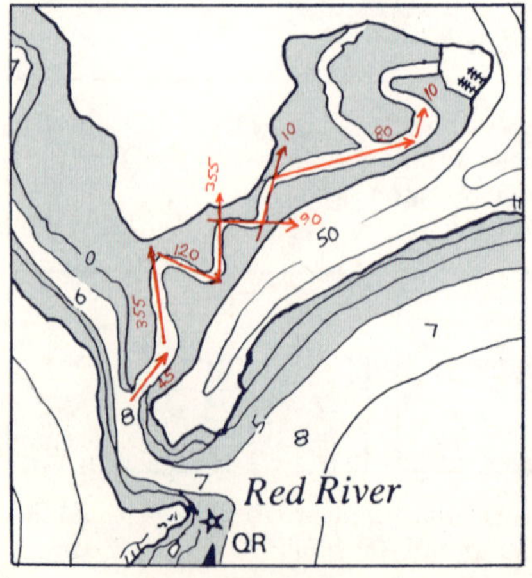

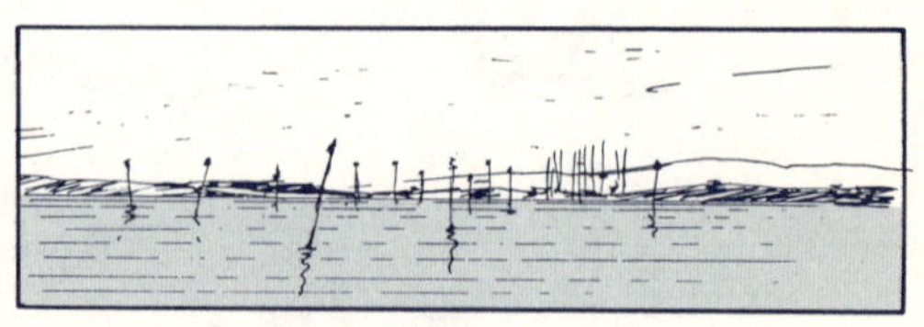

Twisting Channels

These can be quite confusing so note down a few bearings so at least you know where to look for the next mark. If in doubt stop and circle around until you're sure of where to go next. If the marina says it is full for the night and there are no free moorings you'll have to find a quiet spot to anchor.
Ideally this should be away from any harbour traffic and in the lee of the land.

WHERE CAN YOU ANCHOR ?

First, look at the chart to find a good position.

The next Low Water is 1.9m, so you know you are safe over a charted depth of 0m or deeper, with a 0.9m safety margin.

You need to know how much the tide will drop from the time you arrive until Low Water (as you did for *Blue Bay*). Using your preplanned tidal heights, work out your minimum anchoring depth for your arrival time.

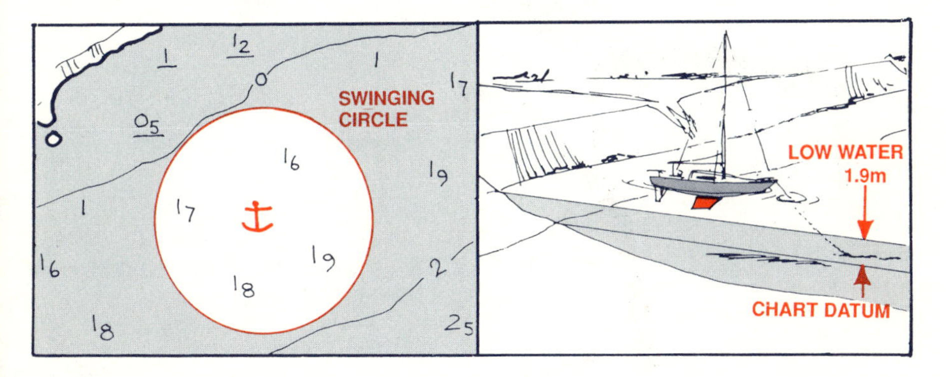

ANCHORING (*see page 39*)

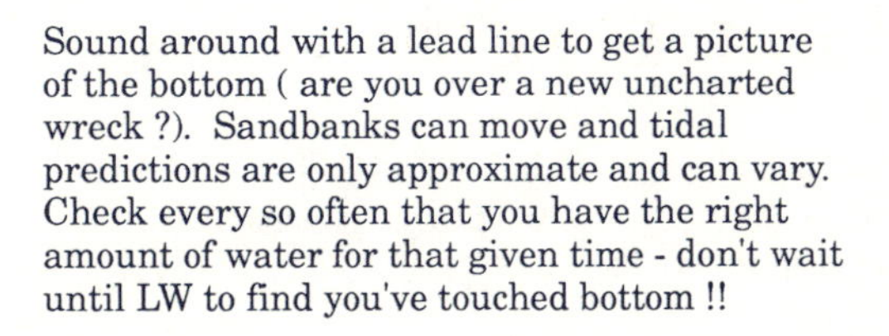

Sound around with a lead line to get a picture of the bottom (are you over a new uncharted wreck ?). Sandbanks can move and tidal predictions are only approximate and can vary. Check every so often that you have the right amount of water for that given time - don't wait until LW to find you've touched bottom !!

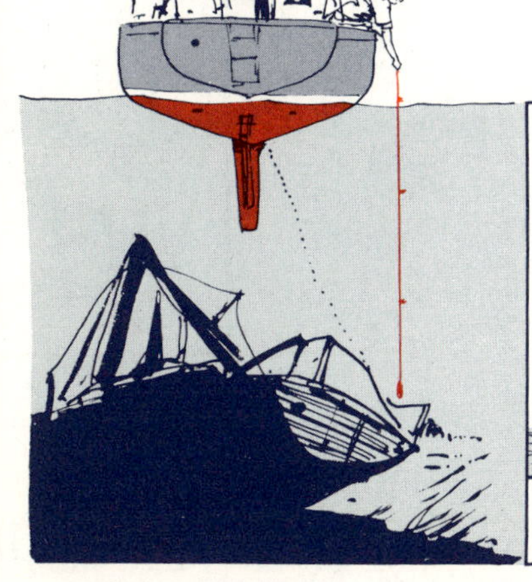

Don't forget to rig an anchor ball by day....

....and an anchor light by night

STEERING

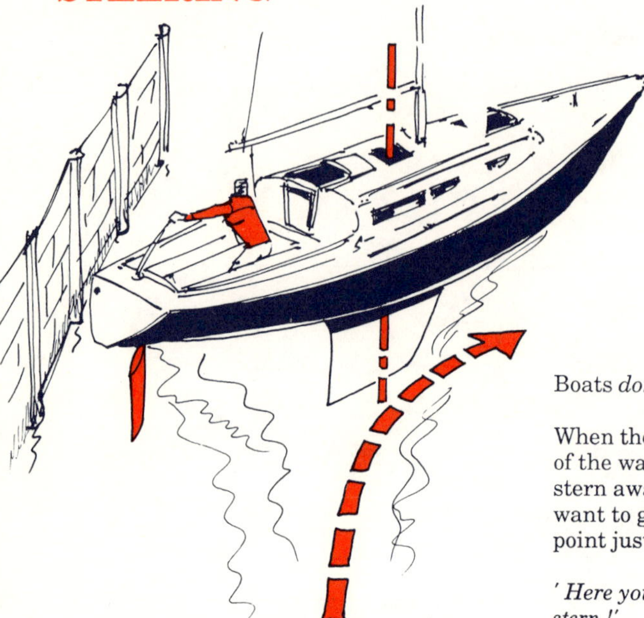

Boats *don't* steer like cars !

When the rudder is put over the force of the water acts on it and pushes the stern away from the direction you want to go. The boat pivots about a point just aft of the mast.

' Here you might hit the wall with the stern !'

PROP. EFFECT

Prop. (Propeller)

Propellers not only push the boat through the water, they also tend to paddle the stern to one side when in reverse.

This is known as the *Prop. effect.*

How to check the prop. effect.

With the boat well secured alongside, put the engine in astern and see which side the turbulence is greatest.

Here the stern kicks to port !

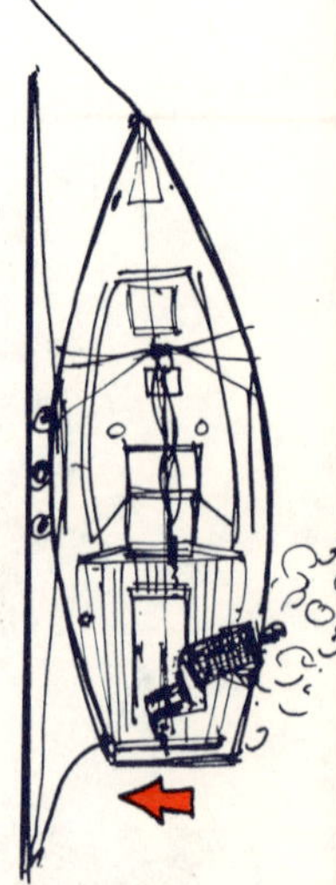

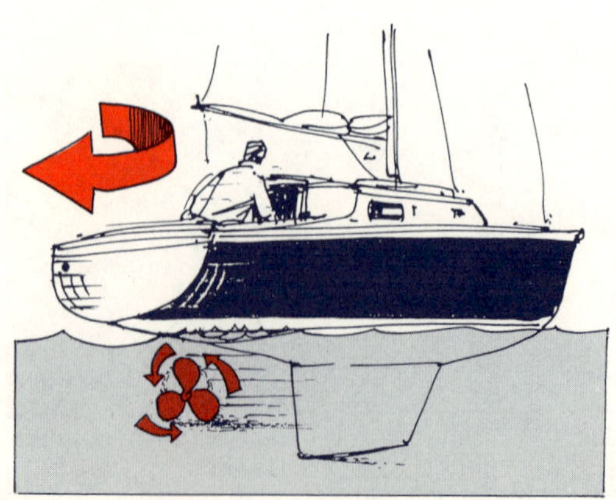

SEE *PAGE 26* TO SEE HOW TO USE THIS TO YOUR ADVANTAGE

WINDAGE

Most sailing boats tend to get the bows blown off downwind as there is more windage there and the front end of the keel is usually cut-away.

But, as boat shapes are all different they are affected by the wind in different ways.

TIDAL STREAM

The speed and direction of the tidal stream has an even greater effect on the boat than the wind.
Always head into the tide when coming alongside, so it can act as a brake....

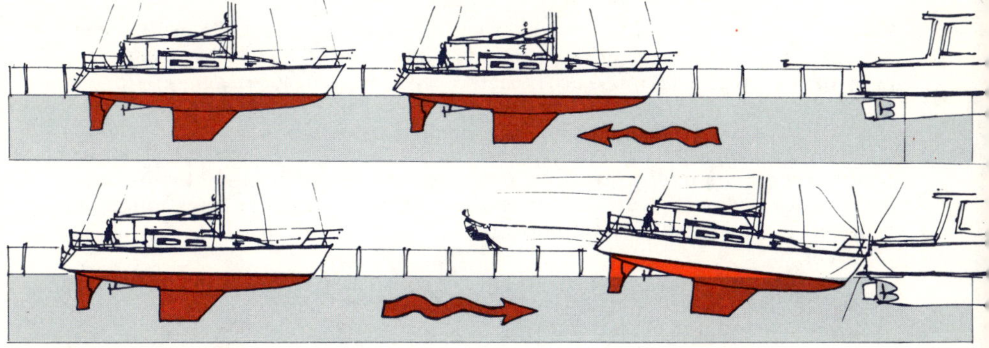

....NEVER come alongside *with* the tide !! (Unless it is very weak.)

RUDDER EFFECT

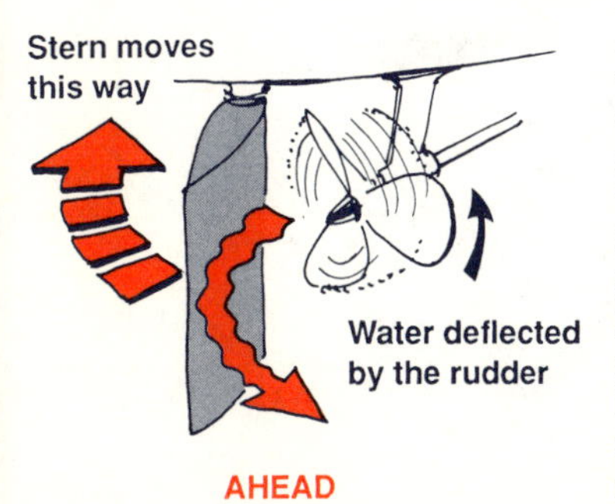

Bursts of '*ahead*' create a prop. wash that increases the turning force of the rudder.
This doesn't happen in '*astern*' as the only force on the rudder is from the backward movement of the boat, therefore the steering is less positive.

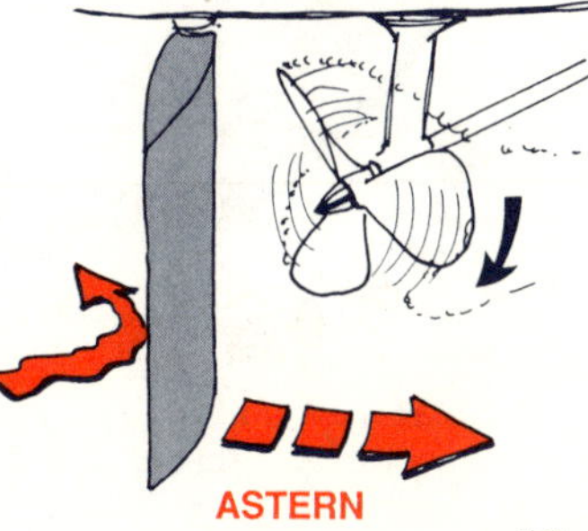

TURNING

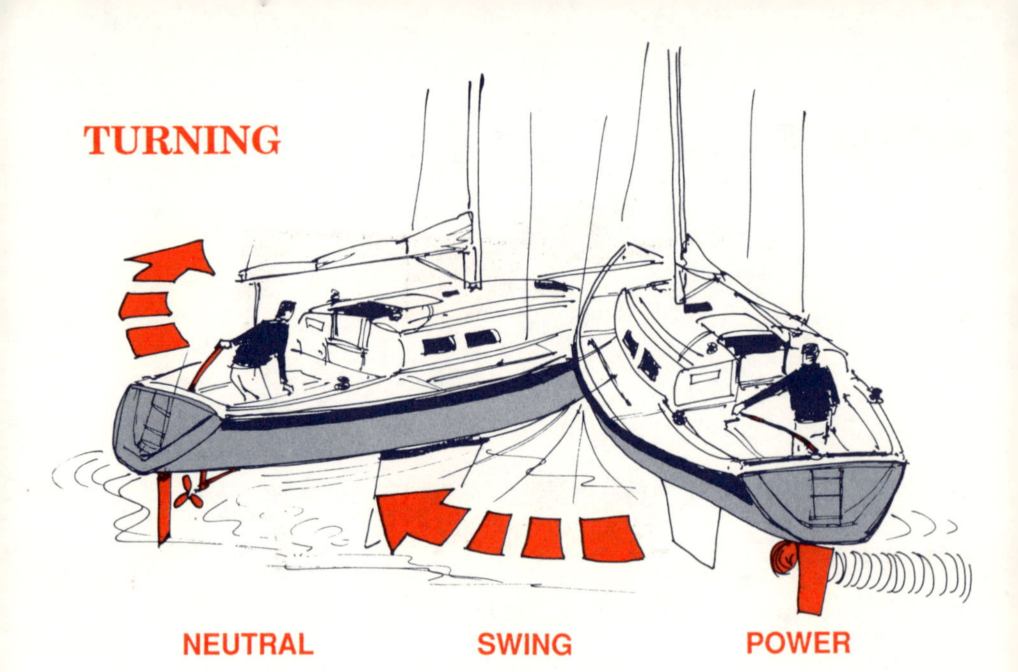

A burst of *'ahead'* will deflect the prop. wash off the angled rudder blade and push the stern to port. Ease off the power and put her into *'neutral'* and let her momentum swing her around. This can be used together with prop. effect (*see page 16*) to turn in a very tight space.

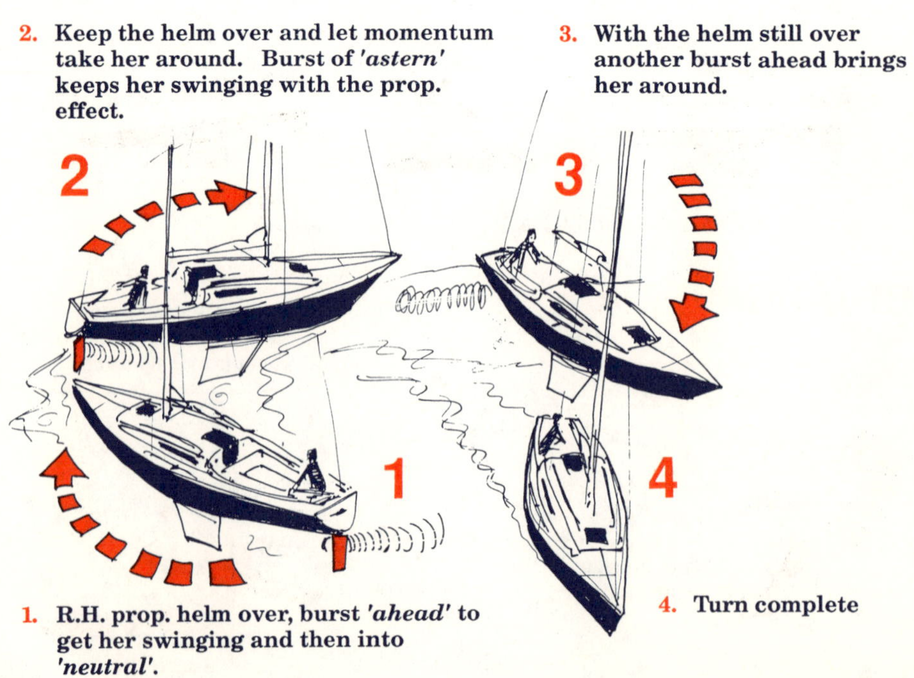

2. **Keep the helm over and let momentum take her around. Burst of *'astern'* keeps her swinging with the prop. effect.**

3. **With the helm still over another burst ahead brings her around.**

1. **R.H. prop. helm over, burst *'ahead'* to get her swinging and then into *'neutral'*.**

4. **Turn complete**

WIND EFFECT

This can help or hinder a tight turn.
(*see page 17*)

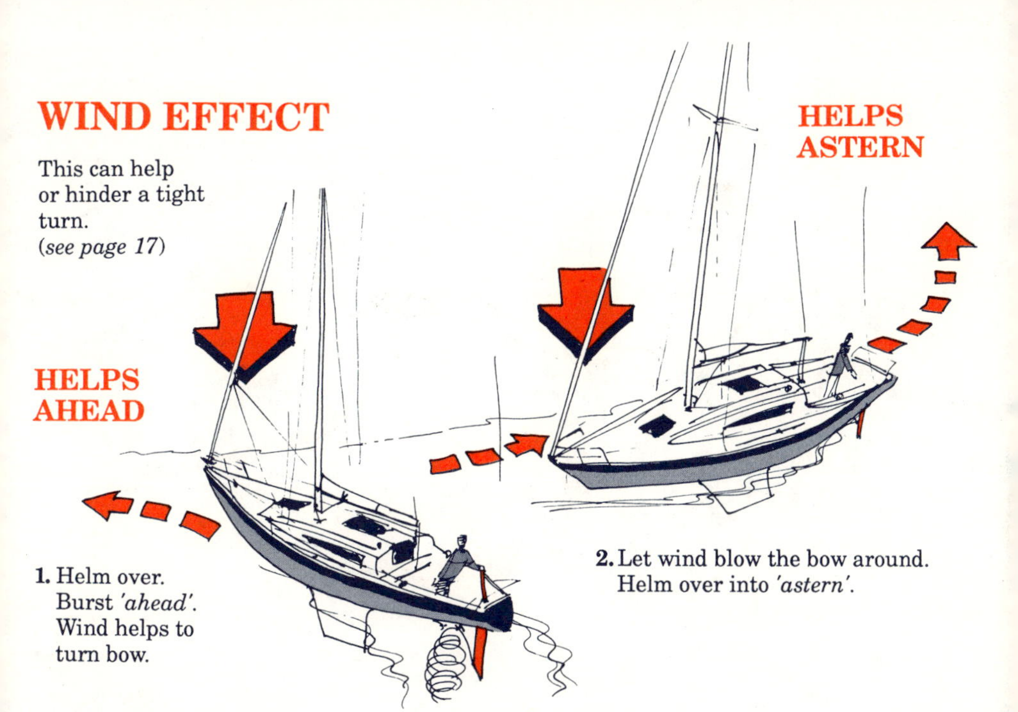

HELPS AHEAD

1. Helm over. Burst *'ahead'*. Wind helps to turn bow.

HELPS ASTERN

2. Let wind blow the bow around. Helm over into *'astern'*.

HINDERS AHEAD

Here we can't complete the turn as the wind blows the bow straight again.

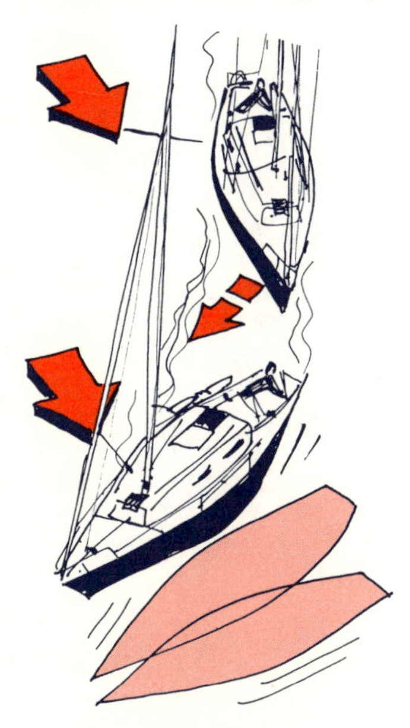

HINDERS ASTERN

Hinders by blowing the bow off, when reversing with it.

Here a touch of ahead is needed every so often to straighten her up.

WHICH WAY IS THE TIDE / WIND ?

This isn't always a simple question to answer.
Assessing water currents and wind directions can be quite confusing, as often the surrounding landscape and shape of the seabed can make drastic changes.

TIDAL STREAMS AND CURRENTS

A. Water flows faster where it is deep.

B. Shallows restrict the speed of the flow.

C. Back-eddies are formed by the shape of the land.

D. Look for clues, like tight mooring lines or...

E. ...dinghies lying to the tidal stream.

F. To check which way the tidal stream is going, stop head to wind and see which way the boat drifts.

G. The flow of the water in rivers and estuaries can be confusing - the tidal stream can be flowing in and the river currents flowing out !

H. The ripples around buoys and posts give a clue.

I. Moored boats tend to lie bows to the stream.

WIND DIRECTION

J. In strong winds moored boats can be pushed in a different direction from the tidal stream - this is known as being *'wind rode'*.

K. Wind direction can be influenced by changes in landscape as well as warming and cooling of the land itself *(see Day Skipper Shorebased Course Notes).*

L. Sails show wind direction in clear air.

M. Look for clues, like flags, for changes in the wind direction.

N. Large buildings can cause *'wind shadows'* (no wind) or back eddies or turbulence.

LEAVING UNDER POWER

To get away from an alongside berth we need to have one end of the boat pointing out into clear water. With a small boat, a push-off with a boat hook or '*well aimed wellie*' will do. But, larger heavier craft need a different technique.

POWERING AGAINST SPRINGS

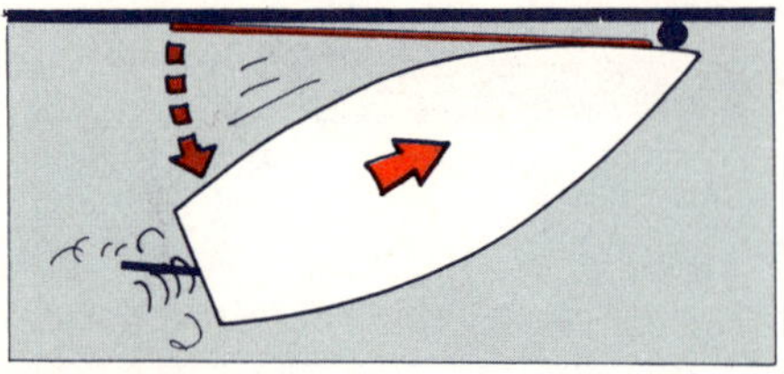

1. Bow Spring
With no tide or wind, rig the bow spring as a slip and pad the bow with a fender. Engage *'ahead'* and, instead of going forward the stern will swing out. Steering towards the wall or pontoon often helps. Then reverse away.

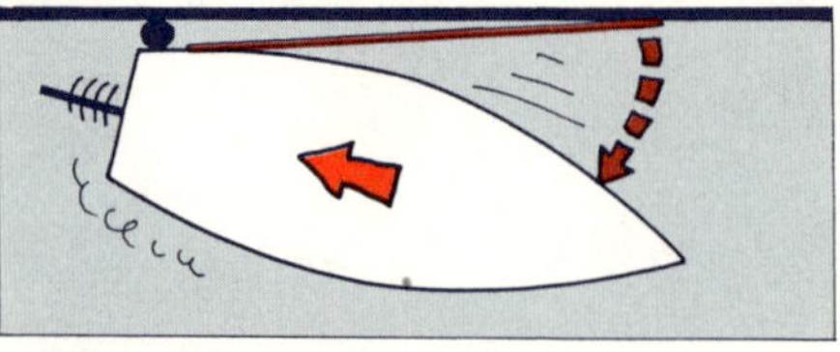

2. Stern Spring
Here again, with no wind or tide, the bow can be made to swing out by reversing against the stern spring. Here the rudder will have very little effect so keep it amidships. When the bow is out enough, engage *'ahead'* and motor away.
Slip the spring and stow the fenders.

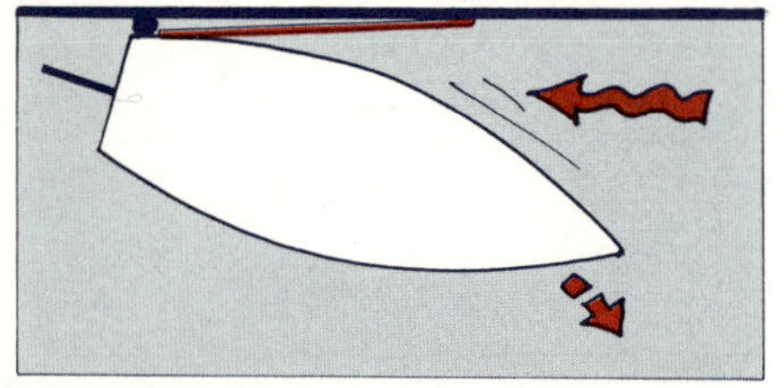

3. Stern Spring with Tidal Stream
By restraining the stern of the boat the bow can be swung out by using the effect of the tidal stream on the bow section. Engage *astern* gently to help.
Motor away in *'ahead'*.

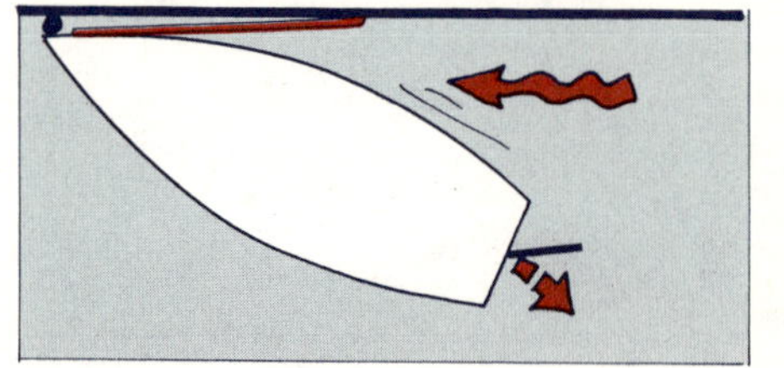

4. Bow Spring with Tidal Stream
Likewise by holding the bow with a spring, the water flow will gradually push the stern out until you are at the right angle. Engage *ahead* gently to help the stern out then gently reverse away from the berth.

5. Offshore Wind
If the wind is blowing off the shore, simply leave the stern line until last and allow the wind to blow the bow out.

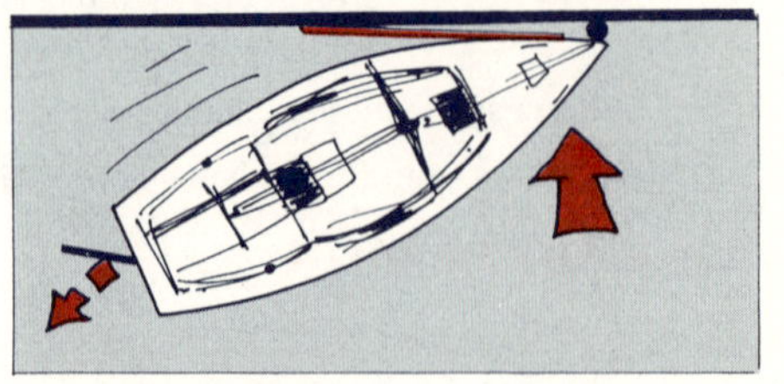

6. Onshore Wind
An onshore wind is not so helpful but combined with a touch of *'ahead'* the stern should swing out successfully.

If the wind is blowing directly onshore and there is no tidal stream it is usually easier to rig a spring from the bow and come away astern.
BUT if there is any tide flowing use it to help the bow or stern to swing out.

MARINAS

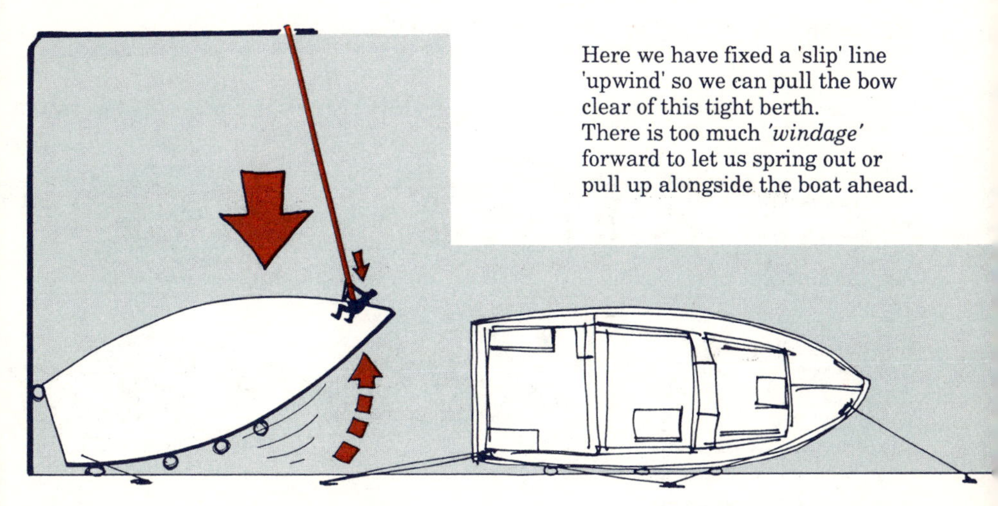

Here we have fixed a 'slip' line 'upwind' so we can pull the bow clear of this tight berth. There is too much *'windage'* forward to let us spring out or pull up alongside the boat ahead.

ASSESS THE SITUATION

Unfortunately real life isn't as simple as text books - wind and currents often being at awkward angles. Try to judge which will help or hinder the situation and then work out how best to use them.
If conditions are too strong for your crew to handle WAIT until things ease off.

Look for clues to give you an idea of wind and tide speed and direction.

Draw them if it helps, and work out how you are going to leave.

Brief the crew thoroughly so they know what you want them to do.

LEAVING UNDER POWER

BE AWARE OF WHAT THE TIDE OR WIND WILL DO, WHEN YOU LET GO THE LINE !

Here a short stern spring (dotted) should have been rigged to stop her crashing backwards.

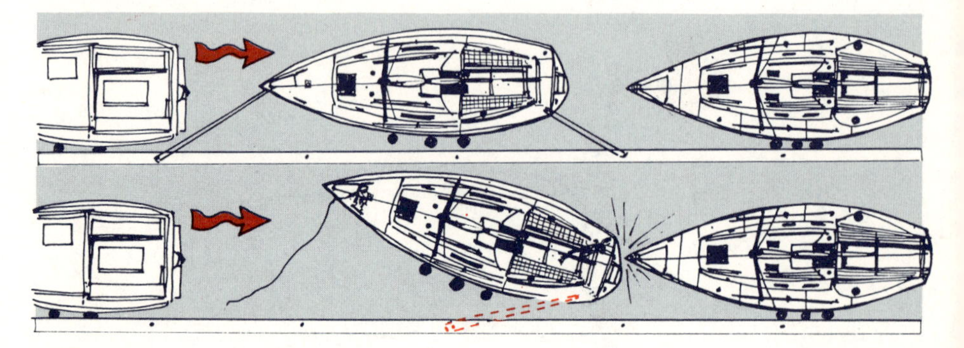

LEAVING A RAFT

A. Here the tidal stream will tear the raft apart as we leave !!

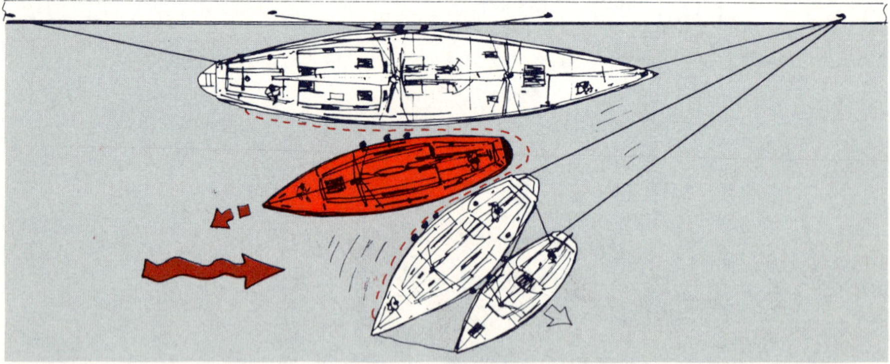

B. Better to rig a new line outside everything (dotted), clear away all your lines and reverse out leaving the current to close the boats together again. Position somebody on the bow to fend off other boats, if needed.

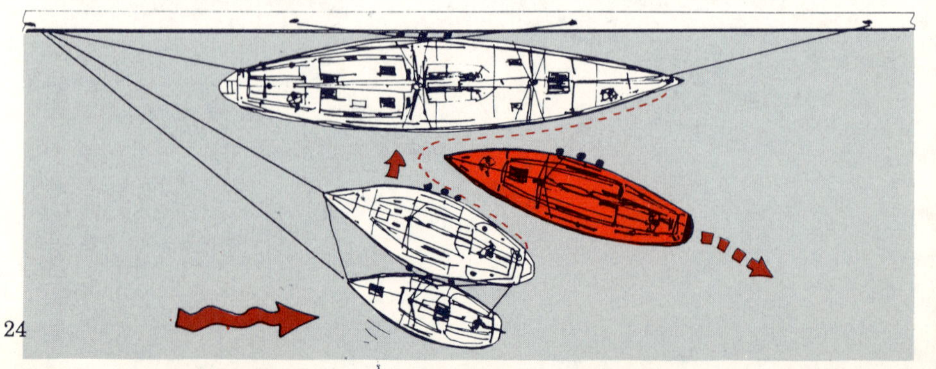

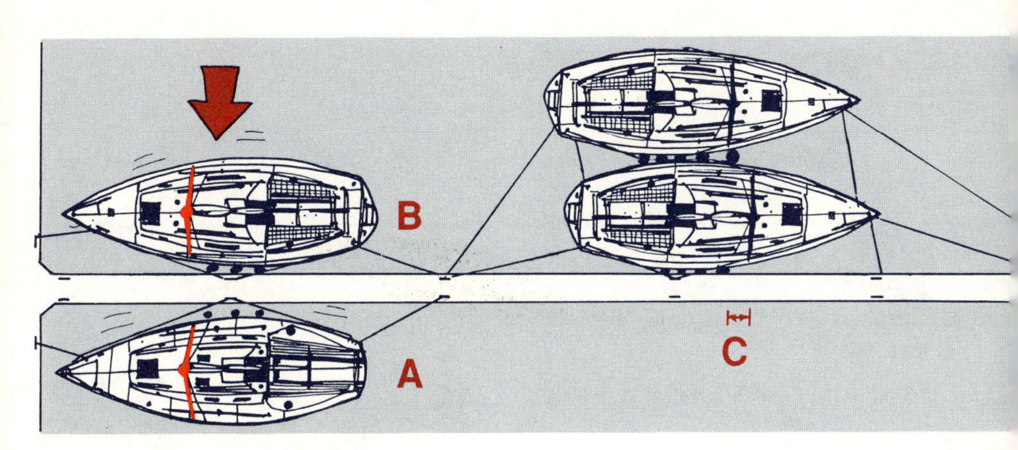

ARRIVING ALONGSIDE

If there is a choice try to choose a '*leeward*' berth **(A)** so you'll be blown off the pontoon - rather than a '*windward*' berth **(B)** where you'll be pinned in with squeaking fenders all night.
If you have to lie alongside another boat make sure the spreaders are well separated **(C)** so the masts and rigging don't fence all night.

1. Brief the crew (which side fenders, lines etc.)
2. Check *'astern'* gear works
3. Look for signs of back eddies flukey winds etc.
4. Make a dummy run and ask permission if you're going to lie alongside another vessel.
5. Check the crew know what to do and don't let them block your view (*see Competent Crew Practical Course Notes*).

COMING ALONGSIDE

Come in at a shallow angle with the longest run up possible.
This will give you a chance to see how the wind and tide are affecting the boat.
Try to be in *'neutral'* so the boat is just *'carrying her way'* when you reach the spot you want.

A. PORT SIDE TO:
The engine should be in *'neutral'* with the boat just 'carrying her way' so a touch of *'astern'* will kick the stern in and stop her.
(*Prop. Effect see page 16*)

B. STARBOARD SIDE TO:
Again, with the engine in *'neutral'* steer slightly away, so a touch of *'astern'* power will straighten her up as well as acting as a brake.

REMEMBER: This manoeuvre takes practice to perfect. The main fault is usually coming in too fast and then applying too much *'astern'* power to stop (*see page 27*).
With a long slow approach see how little power is needed to overcome the tide and wind. This means being in *'neutral'* for a lot of the time - using touches of *'ahead'* to keep her just creeping forward. With experience you should be able to judge how to reach the chosen spot with the vessel virtually stopped.

If there is a strong wind blowing off the pontoon - come in at a greater angle.

The helmsman should stop the boat NOT the crew.

TOO FAST AND TOO MUCH REVERSE

Gradually slow down on the approach, by using *'neutral'* and let her *'carry her way'*. Trying to correct at the last minute by applying lots of *'reverse'* power could cause the stern to swing off course. (*Due to 'prop effect', see page 16*)

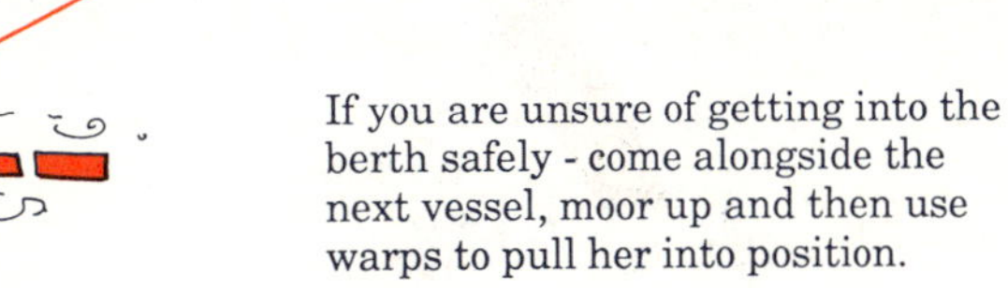

If you are unsure of getting into the berth safely - come alongside the next vessel, moor up and then use warps to pull her into position.

A

If you feel unsure of berthing in this gap in an offshore wind simply motor up to boat **(A)** and attach a bowline.
You are now safe and ready to rig lines to warp yourself into the gap.

IF THERE IS AN ELEMENT OF LUCK INVOLVED IN THE MANOEUVRE -

DON'T DO IT

SAIL TRIM

Sails need to be set up correctly.

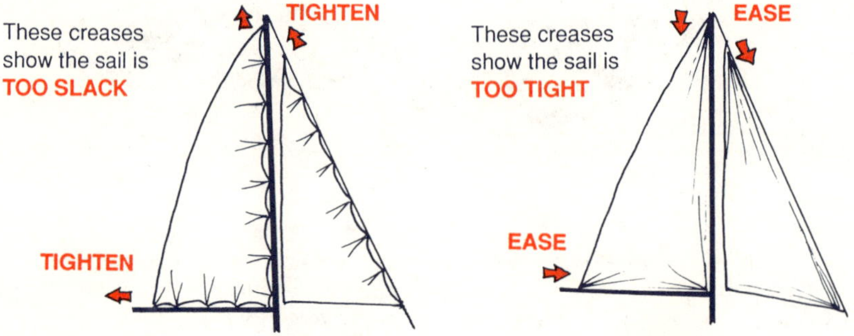

These creases show the sail is TOO SLACK

TIGHTEN

TIGHTEN

These creases show the sail is TOO TIGHT

EASE

EASE

SAIL CAMBER

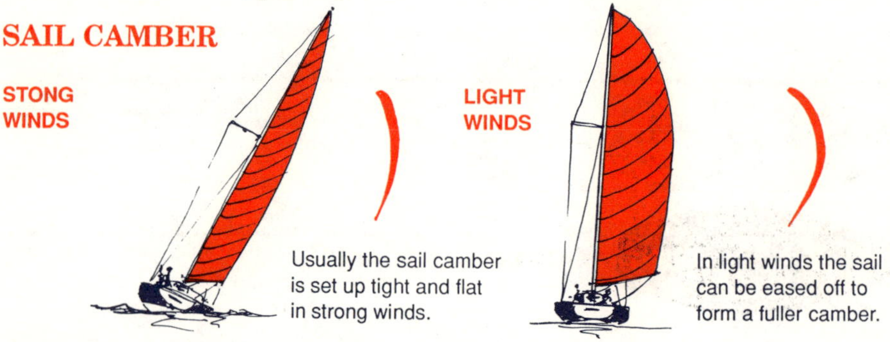

STONG WINDS

Usually the sail camber is set up tight and flat in strong winds.

LIGHT WINDS

In light winds the sail can be eased off to form a fuller camber.

SHEET LEADS

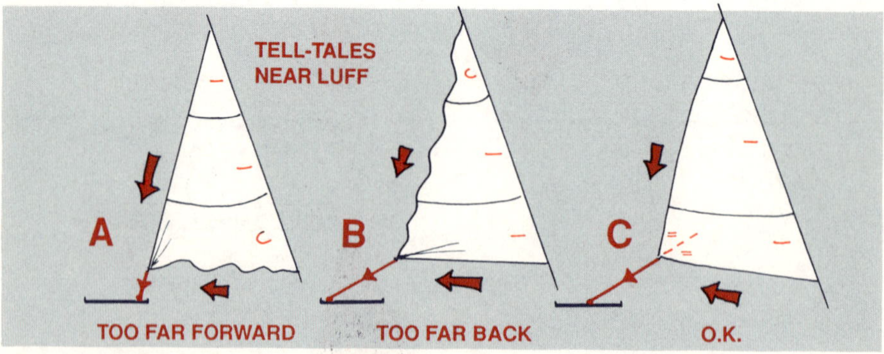

TELL-TALES NEAR LUFF

A TOO FAR FORWARD

B TOO FAR BACK

C O.K.

The angle of the sheet leads can affect the set of the sail.

A. Sheet lead too far forward, leech tension too tight, camber in lower sail too full, bottom *'tell-tale'* lifting.

B. Sheet lead too far back, foot tension too tight, camber in top of sail too full, top *'tell-tale'* lifting.

C. Just right, leech and foot tensions equal, sail camber equal, *'tell-tales'* all streaming nicely (*see page 29*).

HEADSAIL SHEETING

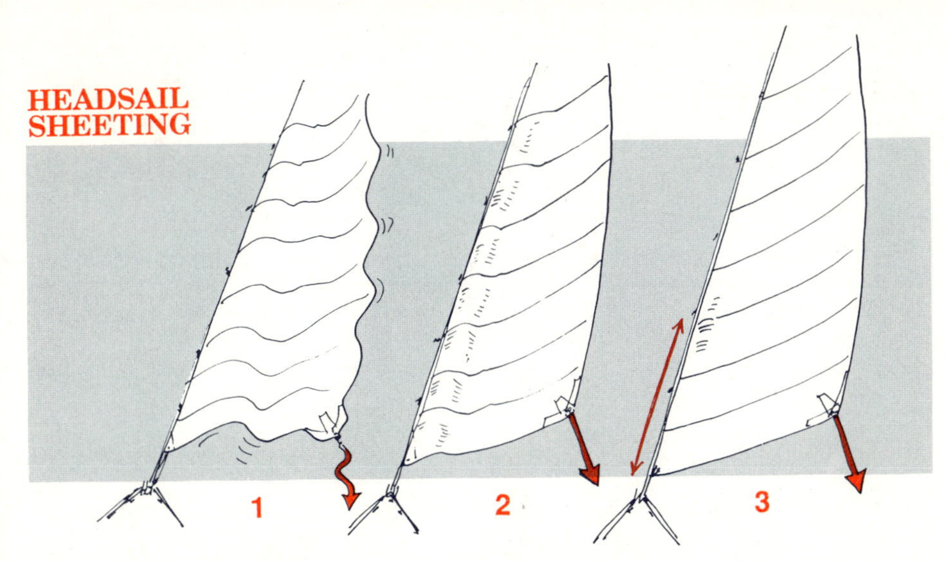

Pull the sheet in **(1)** until the luff is just '*lifting*' **(2)** then harden in until the luff just '*quivers*' **(3)** now harden in very slightly until the '*quivering*' stops.

TELL TALES
(Simplified)

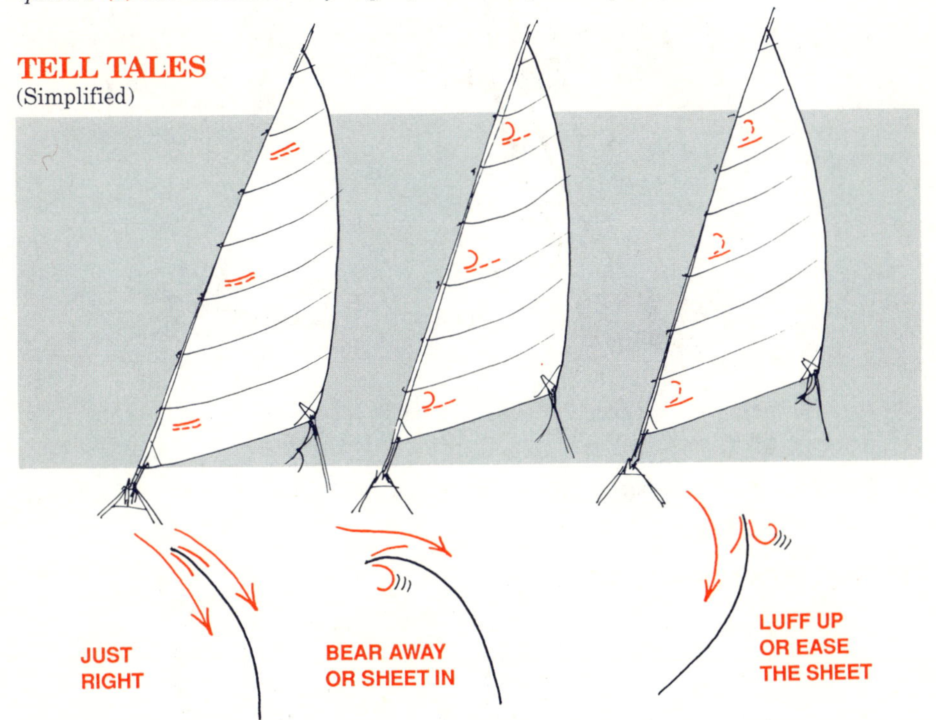

Tell tales are a useful guide to sail trim. They '*stream*' with a '*clean air flow*' but '*flutter*' when the '*clean air flow*' can't reach them.

Racing sailors use them in a much more sophisticated manner.

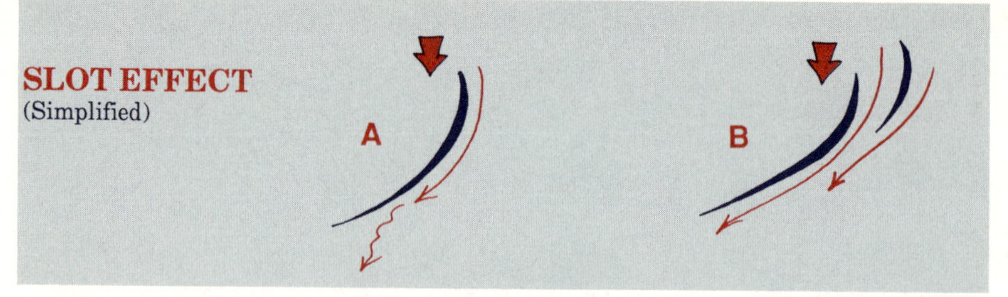

A. When air flows over a single sail it '*sticks*' for a while creating '*lift*' then breaks away.

B. With two sails set, the air flow is modified causing the air to '*stick*' longer over **both** sails. This is known as the '*slot effect*'.

SHEETING AND TRIMMING

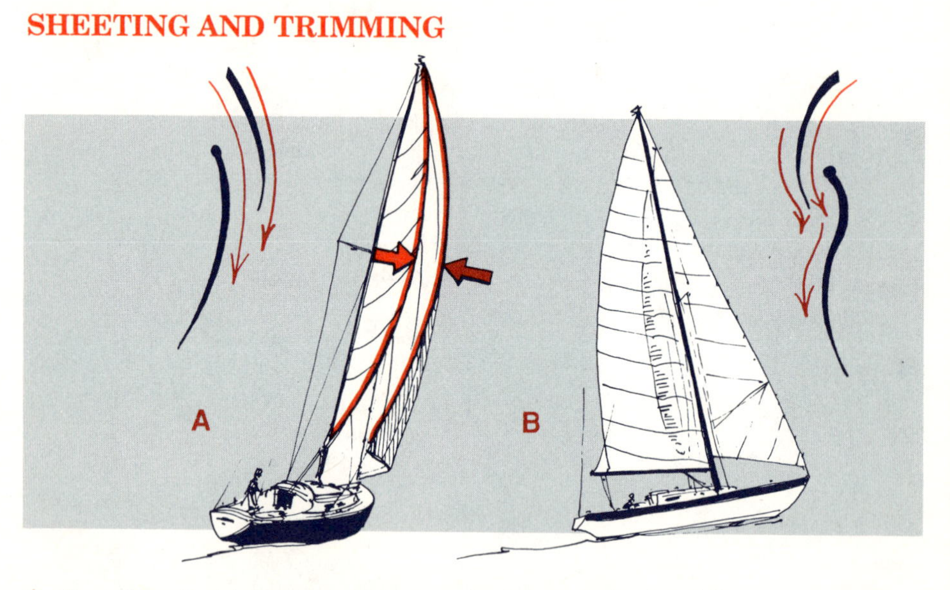

A. Try to keep the '*slot*' between the two sails even so the leeches follow a similar curve. The main needs to be sheeted in slightly harder than the headsail.

B. If the headsail is over sheeted it will disturb the air flow over the main or '*backwind*' it.

DOWN WIND SAILING

As we are not dealing with spinnakers, our '*downwind*' sails will be a '*boomed-out*' headsail, (*see Competent Crew Practical Course Notes*) and a main held out with a '*preventer*' (to stop accidental gybes).

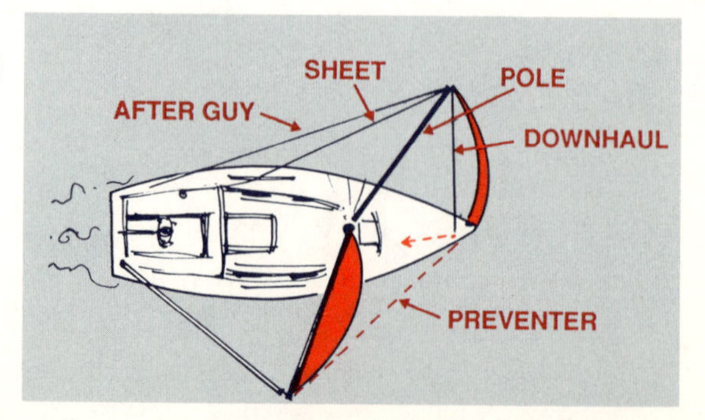

RAISING AND LOWERING SAILS

MAIN

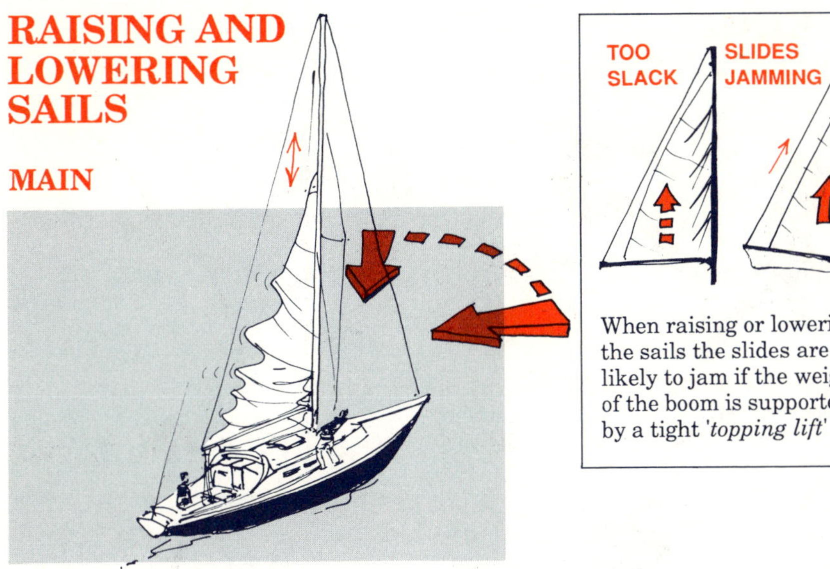

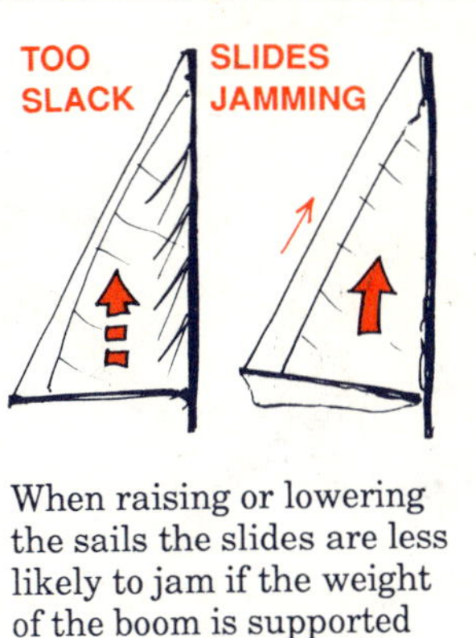

When raising or lowering the sails the slides are less likely to jam if the weight of the boom is supported by a tight '*topping lift*'

The mainsail can be raised or lowered when the wind is forward of the beam like this. It is often worth hoisting the main on a close reach so that the boom is over to one side.

REMEMBER to free the mainsheet and kicker and watch out for battens and halyards snagging in the rigging

HEADSAILS

Headsails can be raised or lowered (handed) on any point of sail. **BUT** if the wind is astern, it is best to '*blanket*' (shield) them with the mainsail. Make sure you have briefed the crew and they know what to do. (*See Competent Crew Practical Course Notes.*)

TACKING

or going about is putting the bow through the wind.

Helmsman says **'READY ABOUT'** and the crew uncleats the sheet, without easing it and says **'READY'**. The helmsman says **'LEE-OH'** and pushes the tiller over and the crew releases the sheet.

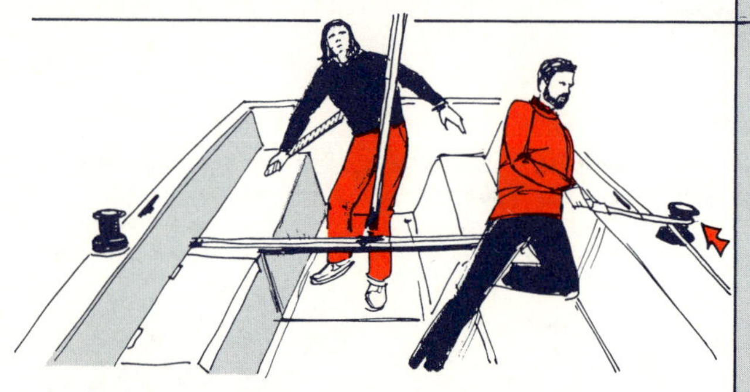

As the boat goes through the wind the crew moves to the other side and starts pulling in the sheet by taking a turn on the winch. The helmsman also changes sides keeping the helm over.

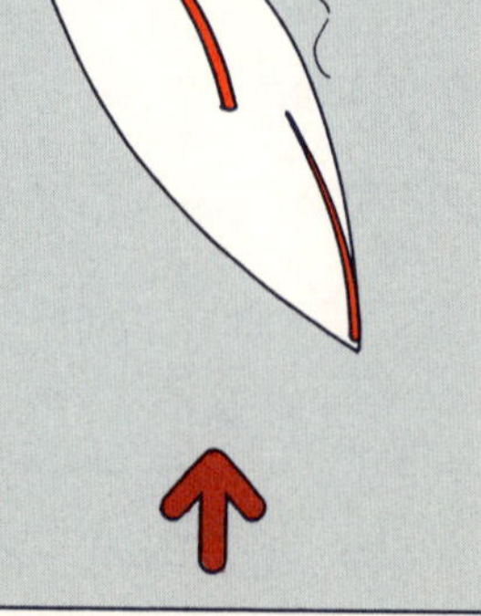

The helmsman can help the crew by slowing the turn (*'giving a luff'*) allowing most of the sheet to be pulled in before the sail fills. Extra turns are put on the winch and the sheet tensioned.

GYBING

Putting the stern through the wind.

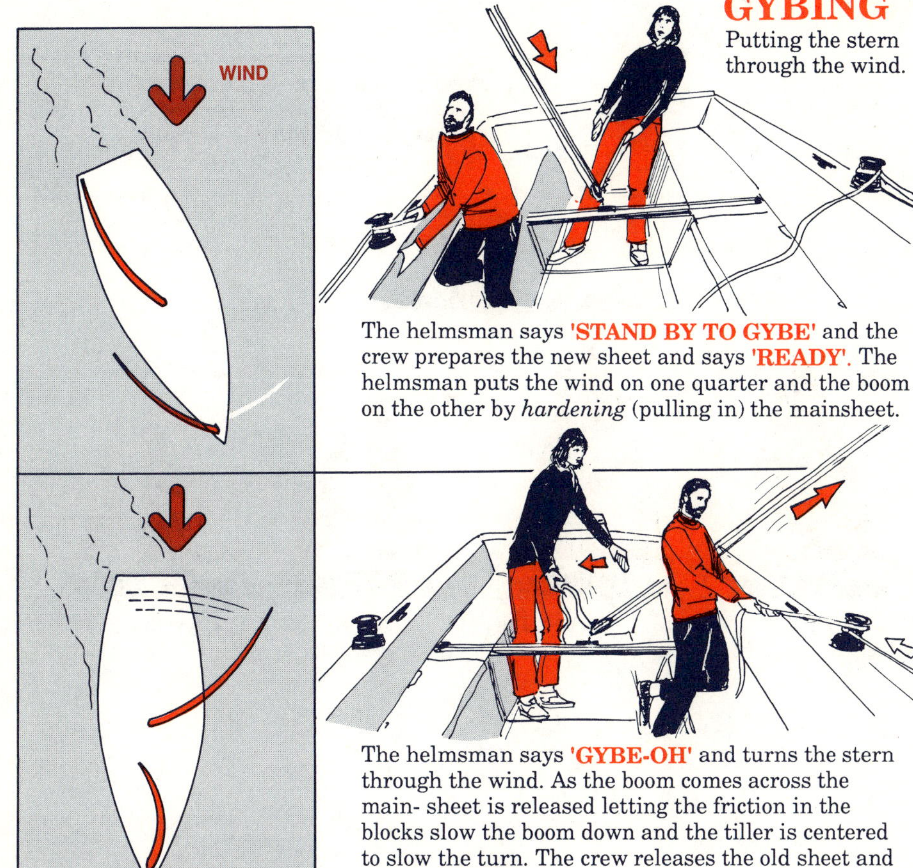

The helmsman says **'STAND BY TO GYBE'** and the crew prepares the new sheet and says **'READY'**. The helmsman puts the wind on one quarter and the boom on the other by *hardening* (pulling in) the mainsheet.

The helmsman says **'GYBE-OH'** and turns the stern through the wind. As the boom comes across the main- sheet is released letting the friction in the blocks slow the boom down and the tiller is centered to slow the turn. The crew releases the old sheet and pulls in the new.

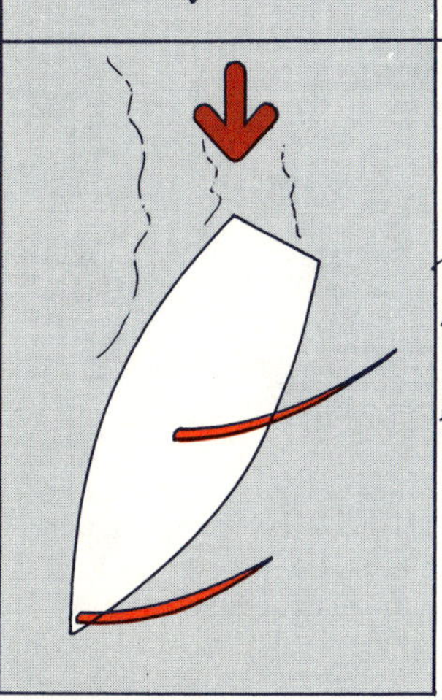

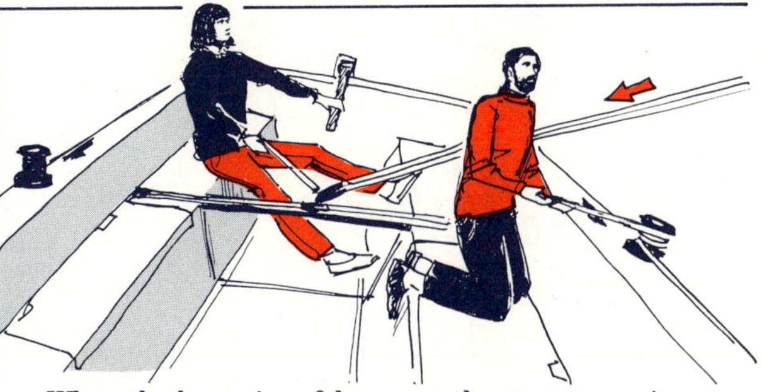

When the boom is safely across the new course is steered and the main trimmed by pulling in the mainsheet. The crew trims the headsail for the new course.

ALWAYS MIND YOUR HEAD AS THE BOOM SWINGS ACROSS THE BOAT.

REEFING

Modern yachts are not designed to be sailed heeling right over. It is faster and more seamanlike to put in a reef and stay upright. Generally if the gunwale is continually submerged you need to reduce sail.

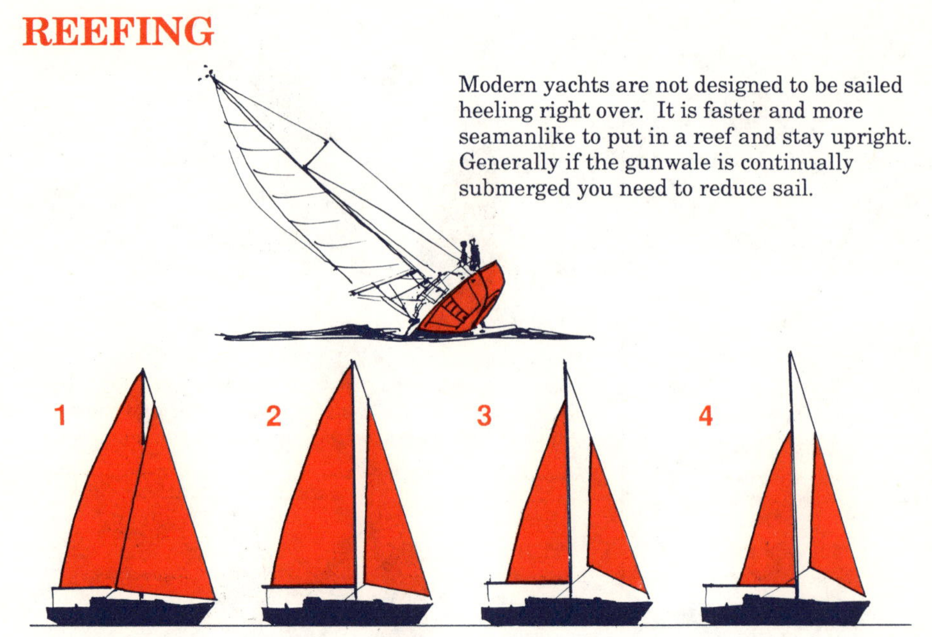

This is the usual sequence for shortening sail. Make sure the sails are well secured and set correctly. This not only makes the boat more docile but is reassuring as well.

If you are expecting strong winds, reef in harbour before you leave.

It's much easier to shake out a reef at sea than to put one in.

The main can be reefed on a close-reach or hove to on a starboard tack - this means you'll be working up hill (*see Competent Crew Practical Course Notes*).

SAIL CONTROL

Most people can sail fast in open water. The hard part is to sail slowly in a confined area.

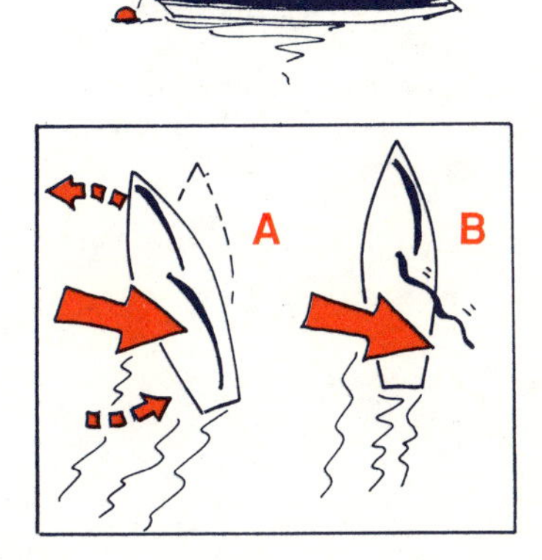

Here a boat is sailing slowly through the moorings and is hit by a sudden gust.
The boat '*gripes up*' to windward and won't answer the helm **(A)**.
What do you do ? ***"Spill the main"*** **(B)**.

The sails are a powerful steering device as well as a driving force (*see page 37*).
The latter can be assessed by **(1)** easing the sheets to slow down then, **(2)** gradually pulling them in so she accelerates and finally **(3)** easing them so she slows down again.
Always slow down on a close reach.

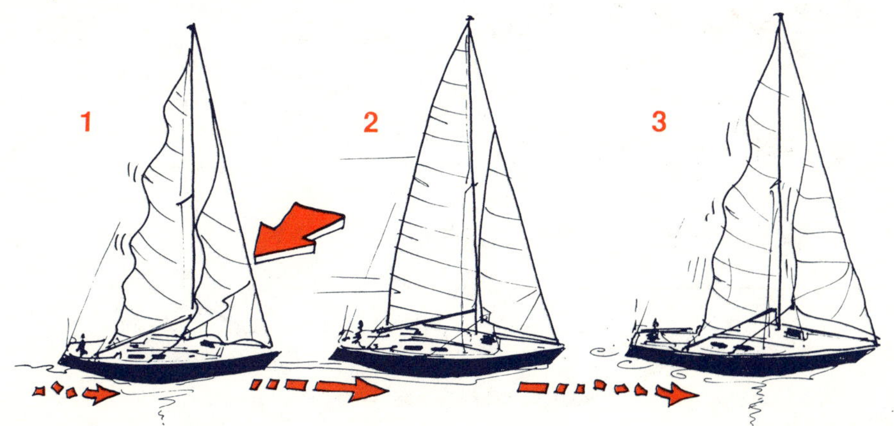

When sailing through moorings keep way on the boat and don't get caught '*head to wind*'.

GETTING THE FEEL OF HER

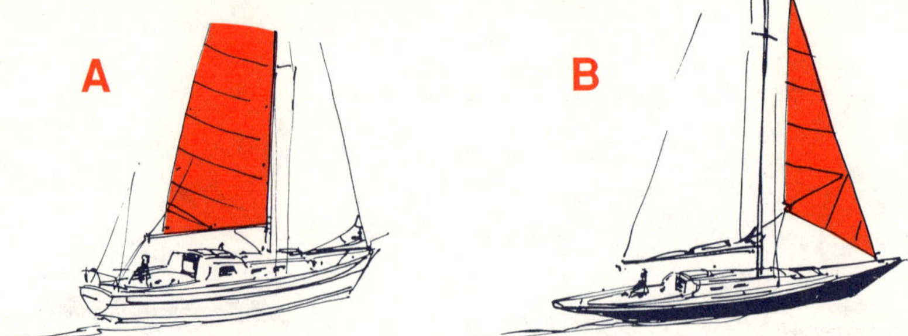

A. How well does she sail under main alone ?
Will she tack in light airs ? How close to the wind can you sail like this ?
B. How well will she perform under headsail alone?

EXPERIMENT as all boats are different.

Sail a 'figure of eight' course with different sail configurations.

See how far she '*carries her way*' when you '*luff up*' into the wind.

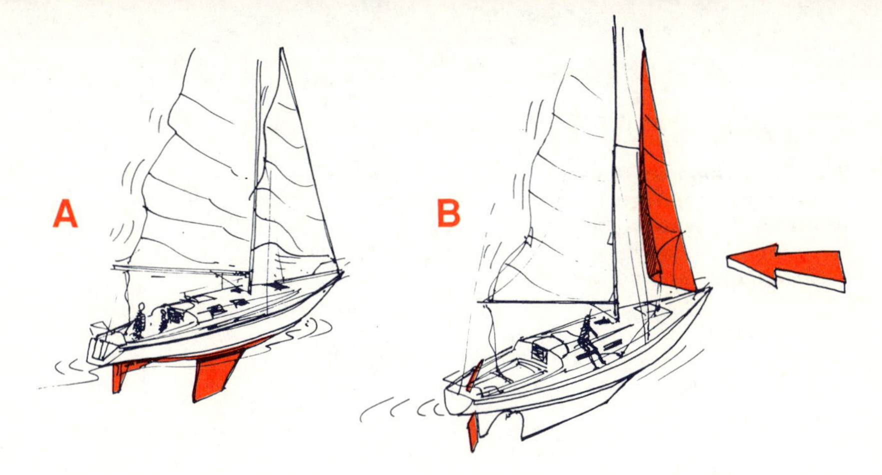

A. Ease the sheets right out and let go of the helm.
Adjust each one to see how she behaves relative to the wind.

B. Can you stop her in the water by '*heaving-to*' with the headsail backed and the helm lashed like this?
Or, will she bear away and charge off unless you partially drop the headsail ?
TRY IT AND SEE !!

The sails can be made to steer the boat :

- **(1)** Let the sails *flap*
- **(2)** Harden in the headsail - she'll turn downwind
- **(3)** Harden in the main - she'll turn into the wind

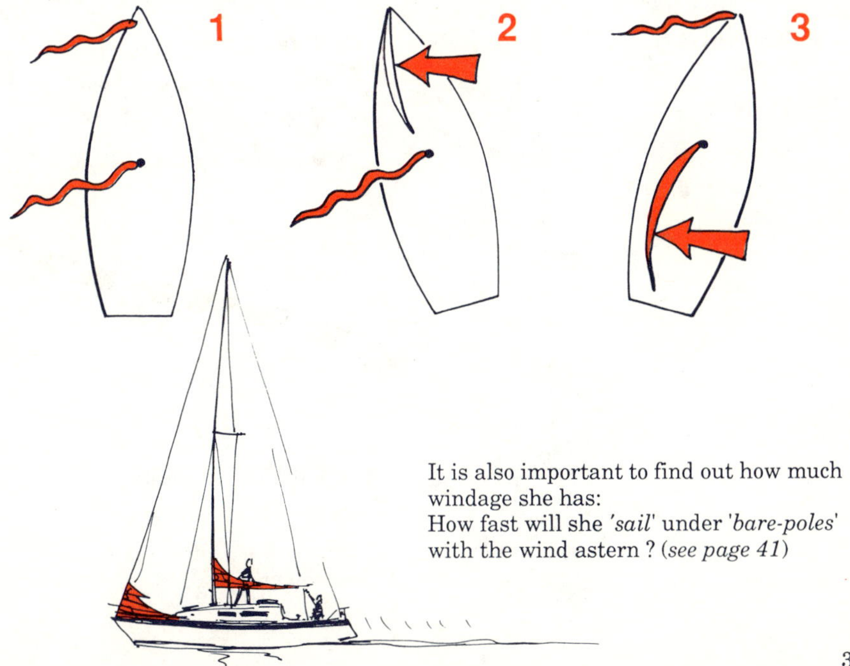

It is also important to find out how much windage she has:
How fast will she '*sail*' under '*bare-poles*' with the wind astern ? (*see page 41*)

CLOSE REACH

This is the best way to sail, in a controlled manner, to a point on the water - be it a mooring buoy, anchor position or man overboard ...

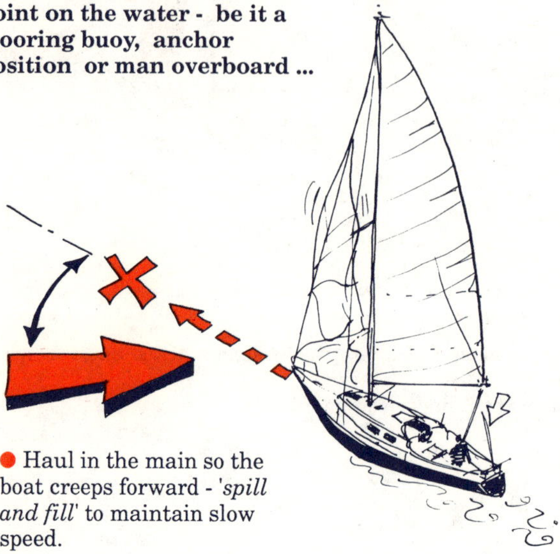

3 ● Haul in the main so the boat creeps forward - '*spill and fill*' to maintain slow speed.

● Let the jib flap unless you need it to punch through large waves.

● Glide to a stop.

2 ● Point at the spot.

● Let the main right out.

● Here it flaps nicely.

● No driving force left in it...

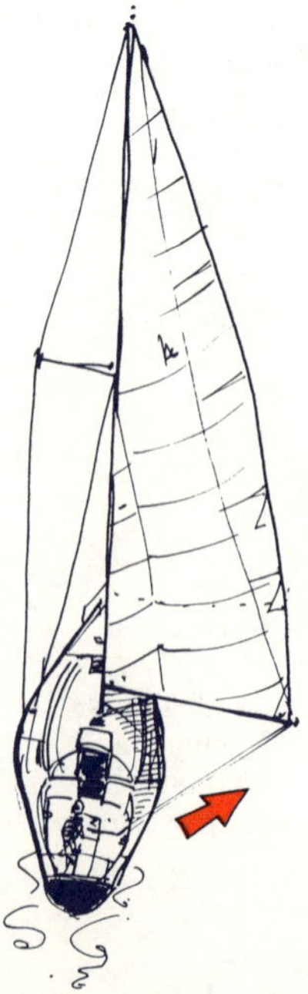

1 ● Point the boat at the spot.

● Let the main right out.

● If it doesn't flap and keeps driving the boat ,'*head off*' down wind...

ANCHORING

SAIL

- Prepare the correct amount of cable (*see Day Skipper Shorebased Course Notes)*. Brief the crew. Lowering the jib helps the foredeck crew.
- Sail on a close reach (*see page 38*) to stop at the desired spot. (If the wind is against the tide, lower the mainsail and approach into the tide under jib or bare poles - *see page 41*.)
- Lower the cable quickly as the bow will usually '*pay off*' quite quickly. Be ready to lower the mainsail.
- When the correct '*scope*' is out '*snub*' the cable (by taking a turn arond a cleat) so the momentum of the boat '*sets*' the anchor into the sea bed.

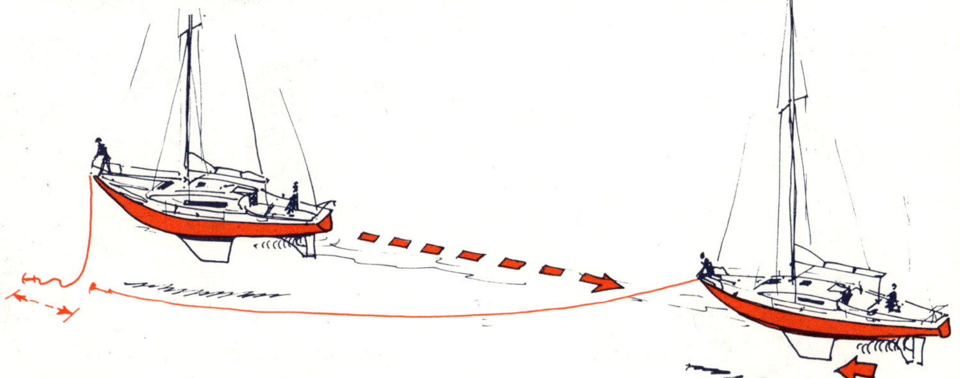

POWER

- When the boat has stopped in the right position, lower the anchor and cable as the boat reverses back.
- Always allow for the anchor dragging slightly before it bites.
- Make sure the cable is paid out evenly so it doesn't lie in a big heap on top of the anchor.
- When the right '*scope*' is out, '*snub it*' and '*set*' the anchor by applying a little extra reverse.

FINDING THE RIGHT SPOT

This is not easy in a crowded anchorage.

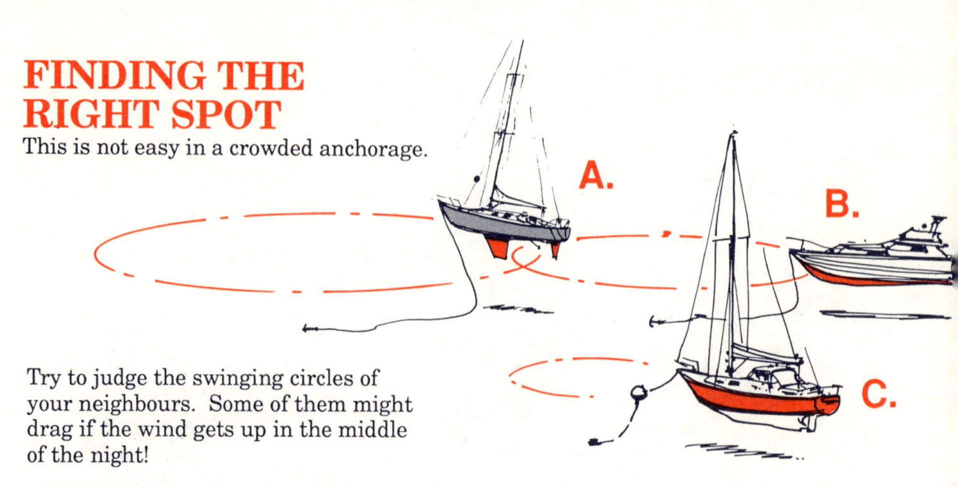

Try to judge the swinging circles of your neighbours. Some of them might drag if the wind gets up in the middle of the night!

A. is a light-weight yacht anchored with rope, so might '*sail*' about in a large circle.

B. is anchored with chain, but also has a lot of windage on the hull and not much grip in the water, so could also '*sail*' about in a blow.

C. is more predictable, a heavy boat *moored* to the buoy.

- Always double check the chart and tide-tables before deciding where to anchor.
- Don't choose a spot like this (*right*) where if the anchor does drag it will drop off the edge !
- Use transits on shore marks to see if you are dragging.
- If you are lying beam-on to the wind at slack water you are dragging.
- If in anyway you feel unsure don't try to put more chain out - get the anchor up and re-lay it.

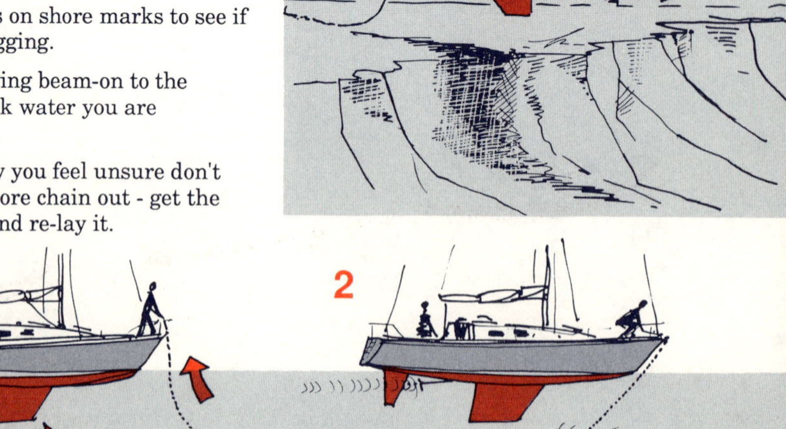

WEIGHING ANCHOR

1. A touch of '*ahead*' will take the load off the anchor cable while the crew hauls it in.
2. If the anchor is stuck '*take a turn*' with the anchor cable when it's straight up and let the momentum of the boat '*break it out*'.

PICKING UP A MOORING

POWER

1. Make sure the crew know which mooring you are after and what to do. Other moored boats will usually indicate which way you should approach.
2. Motor past to check: *Is it a visitors mooring ? Is it in good condition ? Does it have a pick-up buoy ? Are there any stray lines which might foul the prop ? How fast is the tidal stream there ?*
3. Gently motor towards the mooring against the tide while the crew indicates direction and distance by pointing the boat hook like a spear. (*See Competent Crew Practical Course Notes.*)
4. Let her carry her way gently up to the buoy. Again, if you have to brake by using '*astern*' power do it gently so it won't throw the bow off. In windy conditions a more vigorous approach is needed allowing for the wind effect on the vessel.

SAIL

A '*wind against tide*' situation is easy under sail !

A. Simply get the crew to hold out just enough sail to let her creep over the tide.

B. If she only needs *'bare-poles'* and is still going too fast, 'zig-zag' to slow down.

C. Line up shore marks to judge your speed for the final pick-up.

PICKING UP A MOORING

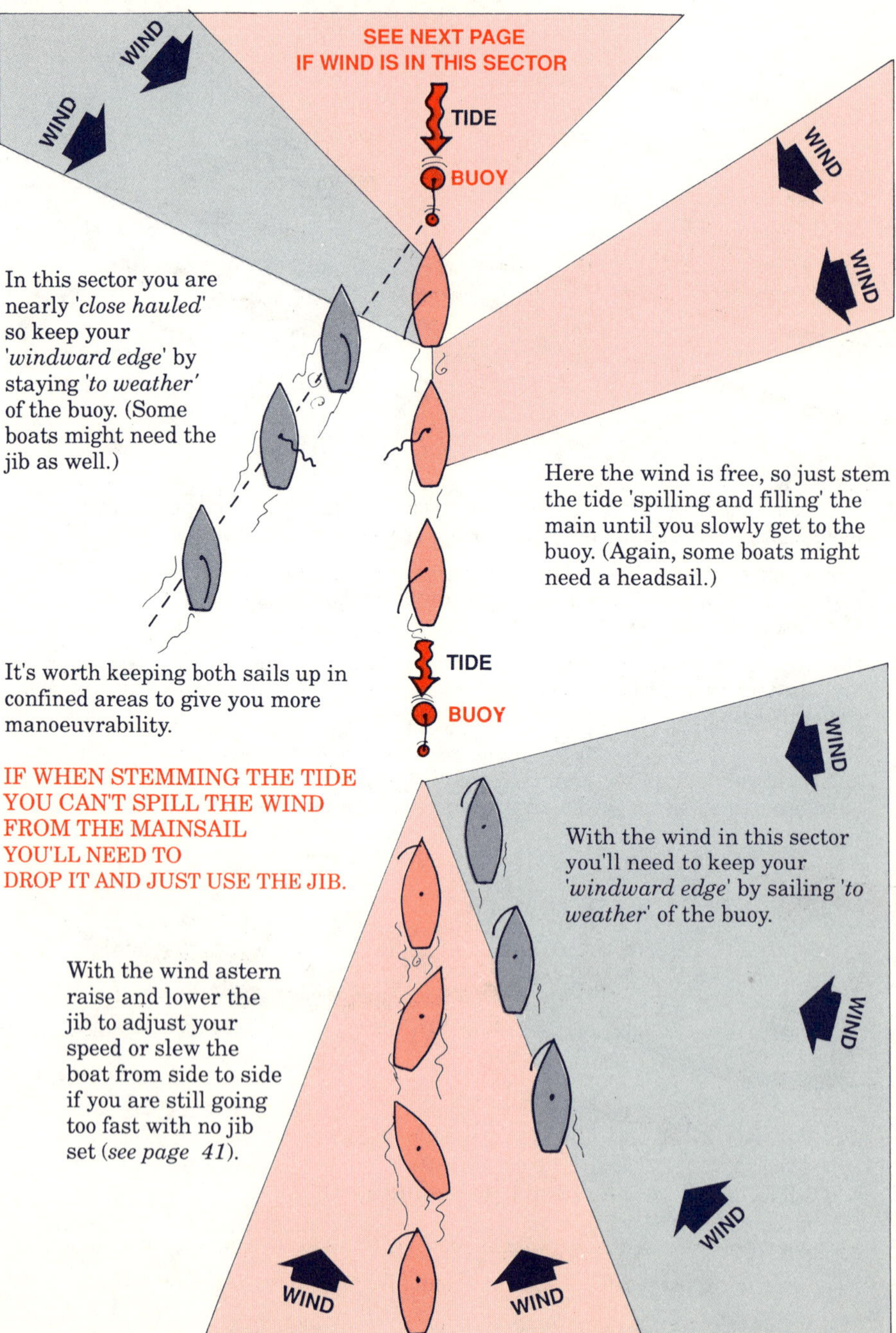

In this sector you are nearly '*close hauled*' so keep your '*windward edge*' by staying '*to weather*' of the buoy. (Some boats might need the jib as well.)

Here the wind is free, so just stem the tide 'spilling and filling' the main until you slowly get to the buoy. (Again, some boats might need a headsail.)

It's worth keeping both sails up in confined areas to give you more manoeuvrability.

IF WHEN STEMMING THE TIDE YOU CAN'T SPILL THE WIND FROM THE MAINSAIL YOU'LL NEED TO DROP IT AND JUST USE THE JIB.

With the wind in this sector you'll need to keep your '*windward edge*' by sailing '*to weather*' of the buoy.

With the wind astern raise and lower the jib to adjust your speed or slew the boat from side to side if you are still going too fast with no jib set (*see page 41*).

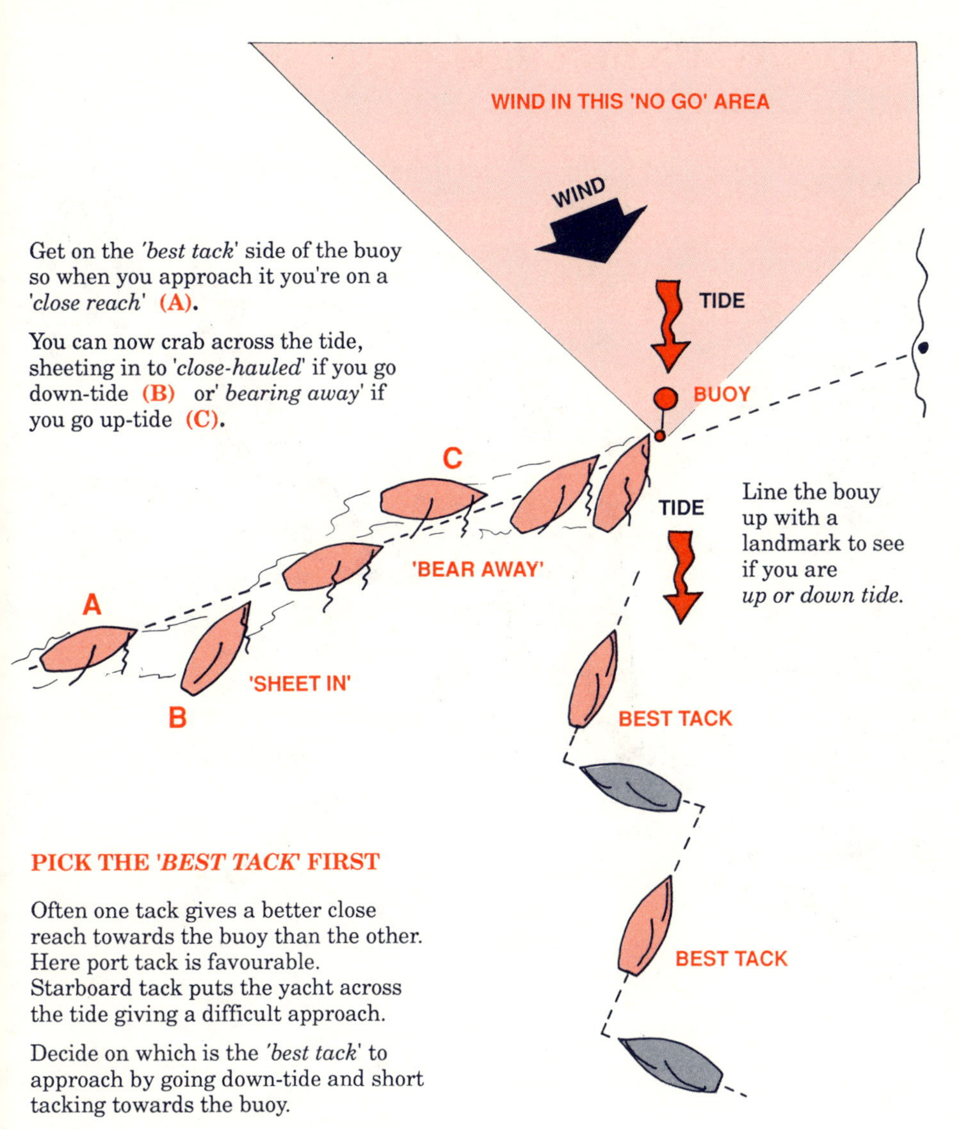

Get on the *'best tack'* side of the buoy so when you approach it you're on a *'close reach'* **(A)**.

You can now crab across the tide, sheeting in to *'close-hauled'* if you go down-tide **(B)** or' *bearing away*' if you go up-tide **(C)**.

Line the bouy up with a landmark to see if you are *up or down tide.*

PICK THE '*BEST TACK*' FIRST

Often one tack gives a better close reach towards the buoy than the other. Here port tack is favourable. Starboard tack puts the yacht across the tide giving a difficult approach.

Decide on which is the *'best tack'* to approach by going down-tide and short tacking towards the buoy.

One tack will usually be better than the other.

Be careful not to steer between the mooring buoy and the pickup buoy.

These pages show the theory but in real-life there are often awkwardly moored boats around (*see page 44*) or other vessels manoeuvring in your way. So, remember it's no disgrace to say "we can't make it this time, we'll have to go around again".

MOORING UNDER SAIL

With the wind and tide acting together a '*close-reach*' approach is easiest (*see page 38*)

1. Sail past the buoy to check it out (*see page 41*).
2. Brief the crew so they know what you intend to do - including your '*escape plan*' ... ... this should be included in every manoeuvre undertaken in a boat "*what happens if it goes wrong* ?".
3. Here we can approach the buoy on a '*close-reach*' from two directions **A** and **B** **BUT** only **A** has an easy '*escape route*'.
4. If you misjudge the approach, tell the crew - **YOU CAN ALWAYS GO ROUND AGAIN !**

LEAVING A MOORING BUOY

POWER

1. Make sure **EVERYTHING** and **EVERYBODY** is ready to leave.
2. Decide which way you want to go and tell the crew your plan.
3. Warm the engine up for several minutes.
4. Have the sails uncovered - just in case.
5. Normally you can just let go and drop back clear on the tide.
6. If you need to leave at an angle, in a crowded area perhaps, get the crew to take the mooring buoy down one side or other so the boat shears off at the right angle. Rig a separate '*slip-line*' back if the crew is weak or the tide is too strong.

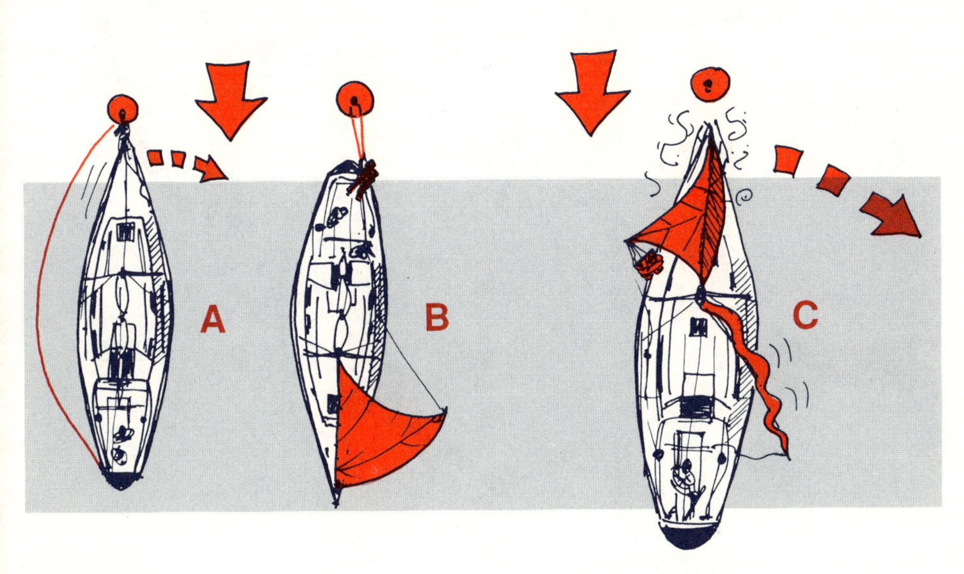

SAIL

A. If you are pointing the wrong way to sail off - simply turn round: rig a '*slip-line*' from the stern, let go forward and pull in the stern line.

B. Let the tide turn you, raise a headsail, slip the stern line and sail away.

C. If you want to sail off, on say '*port tack*', raise the sails, wait until the boat shears slightly to starboard, '*back*' the jib and slip the mooring.

MAN OVERBOARD

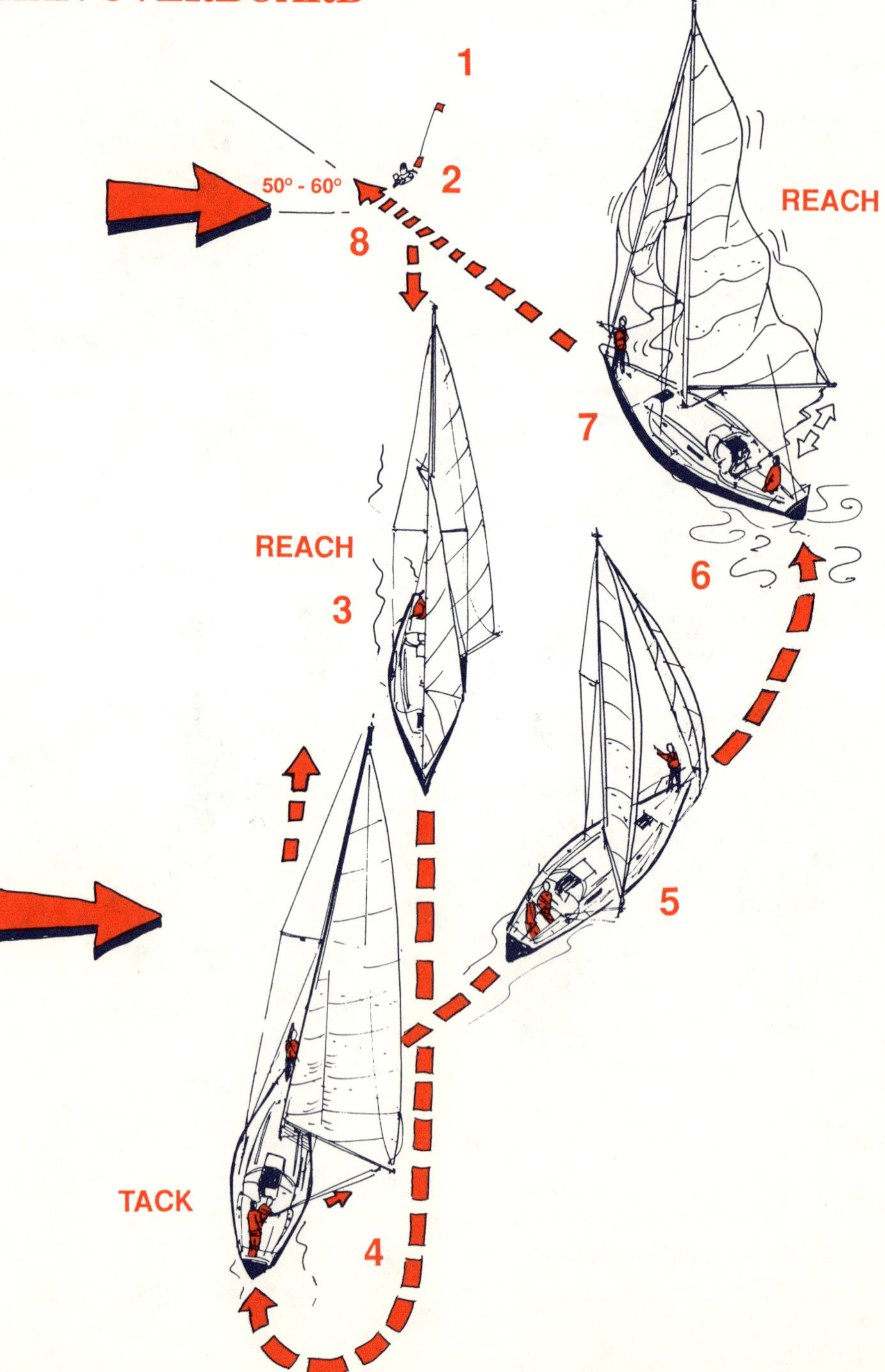

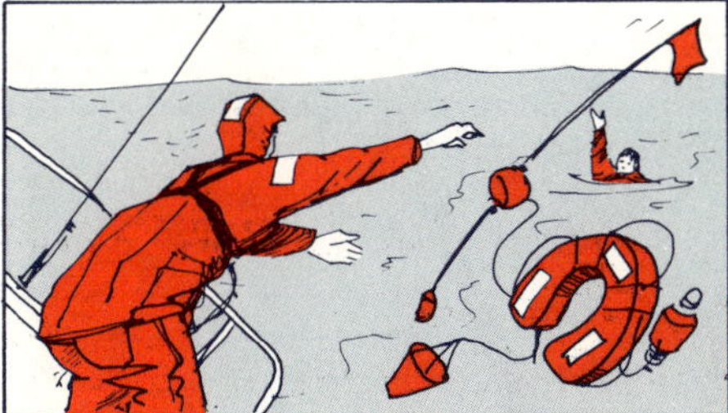

1 At 3 knots he'll be 50ft away in 10 seconds so get the M.O.B. gear over fast. Shout "**MAN OVERBOARD**".

2 Don't take your eyes off him - order one of the crew to keep pointing at him.

3 Position the boat so the wind is coming across the beam (*beam reach*) and sail off about 10 boat lengths.

4 Tack and point the boat at the man and release the main to see if it flutters. If it's still driving as here ...

5 ... turn and sail DOWNWIND quickly. When you think you're in the right position ...

6 look up at the wind indicator point the boat at the man, see if the sails flap.

---

7 Haul in the main and '*spill and fill*' so you can creep towards the man at 1 - 2 knots. Check the speed by looking over at the passing water.

You'll only need the headsail to punch through big waves so let it flap.

Approach at about 50° - 60° to the wind aiming about 6ft to windward of the casualty (*see page 38*).

Remember, as you slow down the wind and waves will push you sideways.

8 Stop by him - some people like to haul the main in tight to make the boat luff up slightly - it all depends on the boat.

MAN OVERBOARD

QUICK STOP WITH ENGINE

'*Heave-to*', start the engine and drop or roll-up the headsail.

Make sure no lines are trailing overboard.

Haul in the mainsheet tight. Mind the *gybe*.

Motor DOWNWIND, turn and approach the casualty with your wind indicator pointing at the man overboard and the mainsail flapping amidships.

IT IS OFTEN WORTH TACKING TO *'HEAVE TO'* IMMEDIATELY ESPECIALLY AT NIGHT. YOU CAN THEN DECIDE WHETHER TO APPROACH UNDER SAIL OR POWER (OR BOTH).

GETTING HIM BACK

It's safer in choppy conditions to make contact with some form of floating pick-up line rather than getting the boat too close.

In warm water he'll probably be able to use a boarding ladder - but it is safer in large seas to rig it securely amidships.

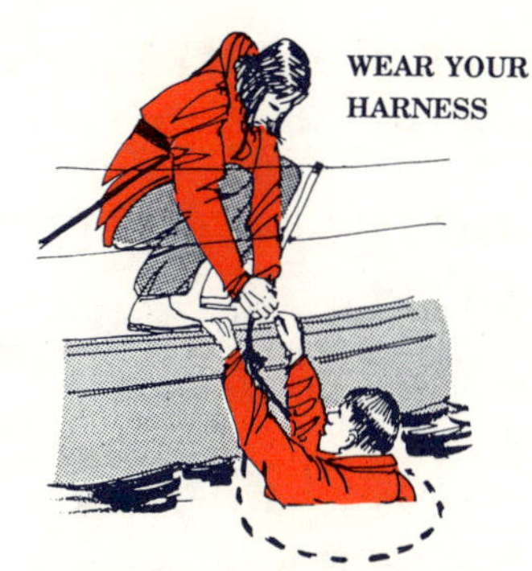

ALWAYS TIE HIM TO THE BOAT FIRST before trying to get him out.

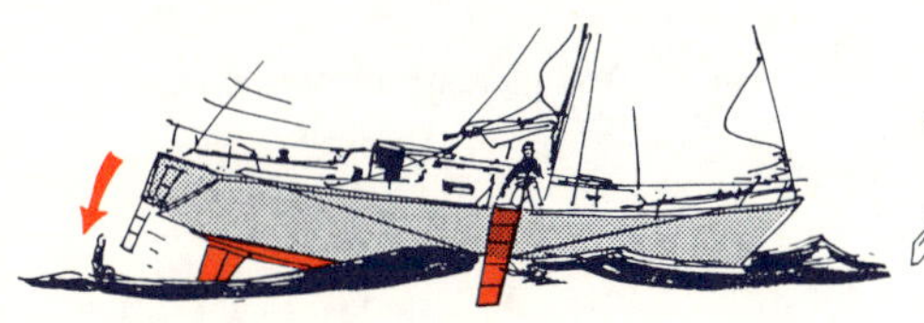

After only a matter of minutes, in cold water, the casualty won't be able to help himself - so some form of pre-arranged '*crane*' must be used.

A half-inflated dinghy has been used to drag the man out of the water BUT it's not easy !

Here a 6:1 block and tackle is left permanently rigged to a spare halyard. The fall is lead back to a winch via the genoa car.

Here the boom has been '*guyed*' fore and aft and the powerful mainsheet used to lift the casualty.
Once up the boom can be used to swing him inboard and down the mainhatch.

If the victim is unconscious, a crew member might have to go into the water to help him. He MUST wear a life-jacket and be attached to the boat with a strong line.
The '*kiss of life*' can be given in the water.

WET PEOPLE ARE **EXTREMELY** HEAVY - SO WORK OUT A 'CRANE' SYSTEM THAT WILL WORK ON YOUR BOAT.

VHF RADIO DISTRESS CALL

A distress call is sent when there is *GRAVE AND IMMINENT DANGER* to a vessel or person and *IMMEDIATE ASSISTANCE* is required.

HOW TO SEND A DISTRESS CALL.

Switch on power, switch on radio, select *CH16*, turn to high power. Push press-to-transmit switch and speak slowly and distinctly.

- MAYDAY, MAYDAY, MAYDAY.
- This is (Yacht's Name 3 times)
- MAYDAY (Yacht's Name)
- Position (see below)
- Nature of distress
- Any extra information which might help
- Over
- Take your finger off the transmit button

Turning on the set etc can be forgotten in an emergency so make up a reminder card and stick it up near the radio.

MAYDAY is the international distress signal.

The 'name' and the word 'yacht' helps the searchers know what they are looking for.

"I require immediate assistance" and include number of people on board, whether you are going to abandon ship or have fired flares etc.

'Over' means please reply.

AN URGENCY CALL

An urgency call is used when you have a *VERY IMPORTANT MESSAGE* to send covering *SAFETY*.

PAN PAN, PAN PAN, PAN PAN,
All stations (3 times)
this is (Yacht's name 3 times)

- Position
- Nature of urgency
- Assistance required
- Over

The advantage of an urgency call is that it lets the world know you are in some sort of trouble without launching all the rescue services at that moment.

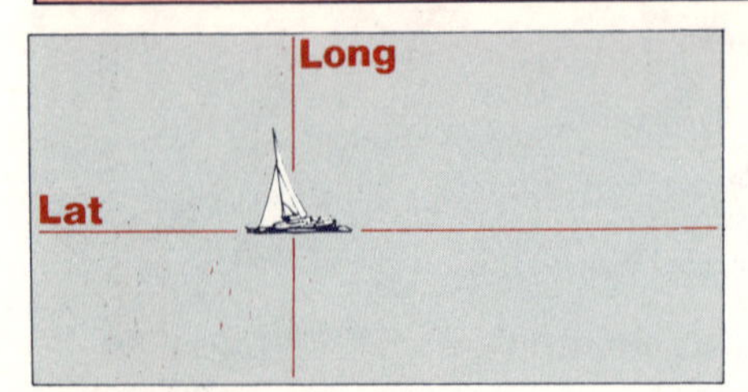

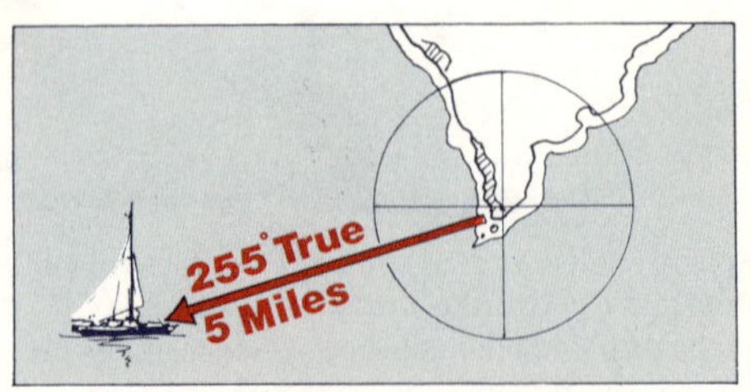

POSITIONS MUST BE GIVEN IN LAT. LONG. OR TRUE BEARINGS **FROM A** WELL DEFINED CHARTED POSITION WITH DISTANCE OFF. (e g Position 255° from South Head, 5 miles.)

If it is onboard, an Emergency Position Indicating Radio Beacon (or EPIRB) should be activated to raise the alarm and help the rescue services home in on you.
(See page 55 for MEDICAL ADVICE BY RADIO)

DISTRESS SIGNALS

Marine pyrotechnics are a simple way of sending a distress signal.
Make sure all the crew know how to fire them.
This is the *minimum* you should carry.

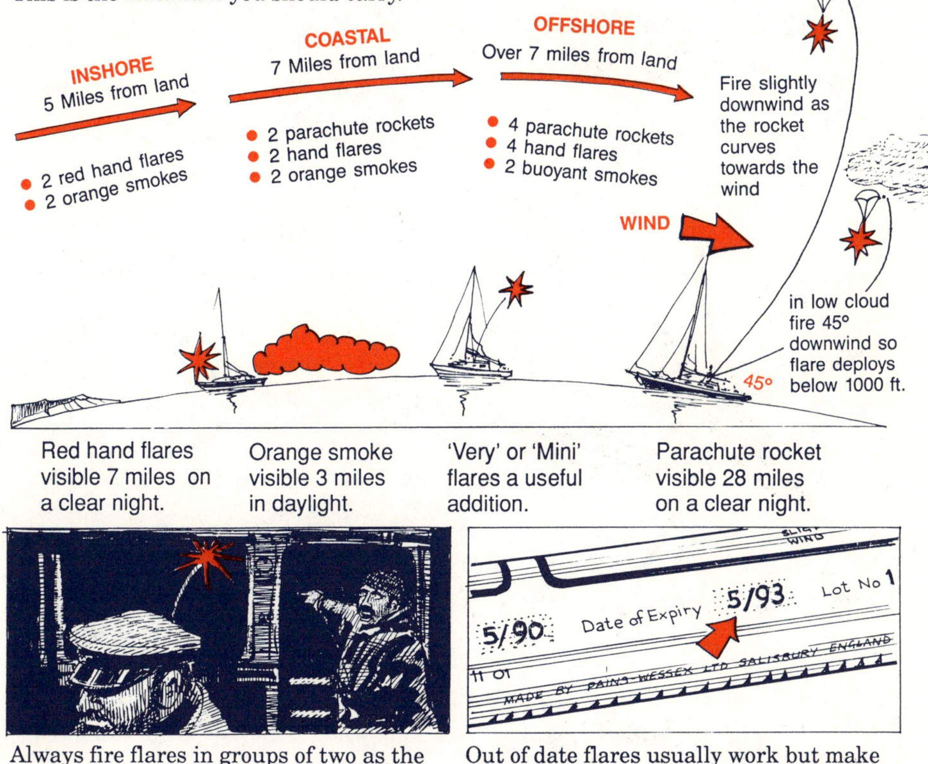

Always fire flares in groups of two as the first one might be missed by the person in charge of a potential rescue vessel.

Out of date flares usually work but make sure there are always enough new ones on board and inspect for signs of deterioration.

OTHER SIGNALS FOR HELP

Slowly raising and lowering your arms

A ball over or under a square shape works continuously and can be seen in poor light at long distances.

The signal **NC** can be made by flags.

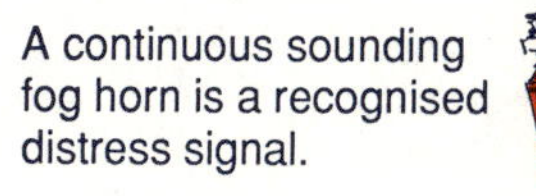

A continuous sounding fog horn is a recognised distress signal.

S.O.S. sent by any means

The signal 'V' means "I require assistance"
(not a distress signal)

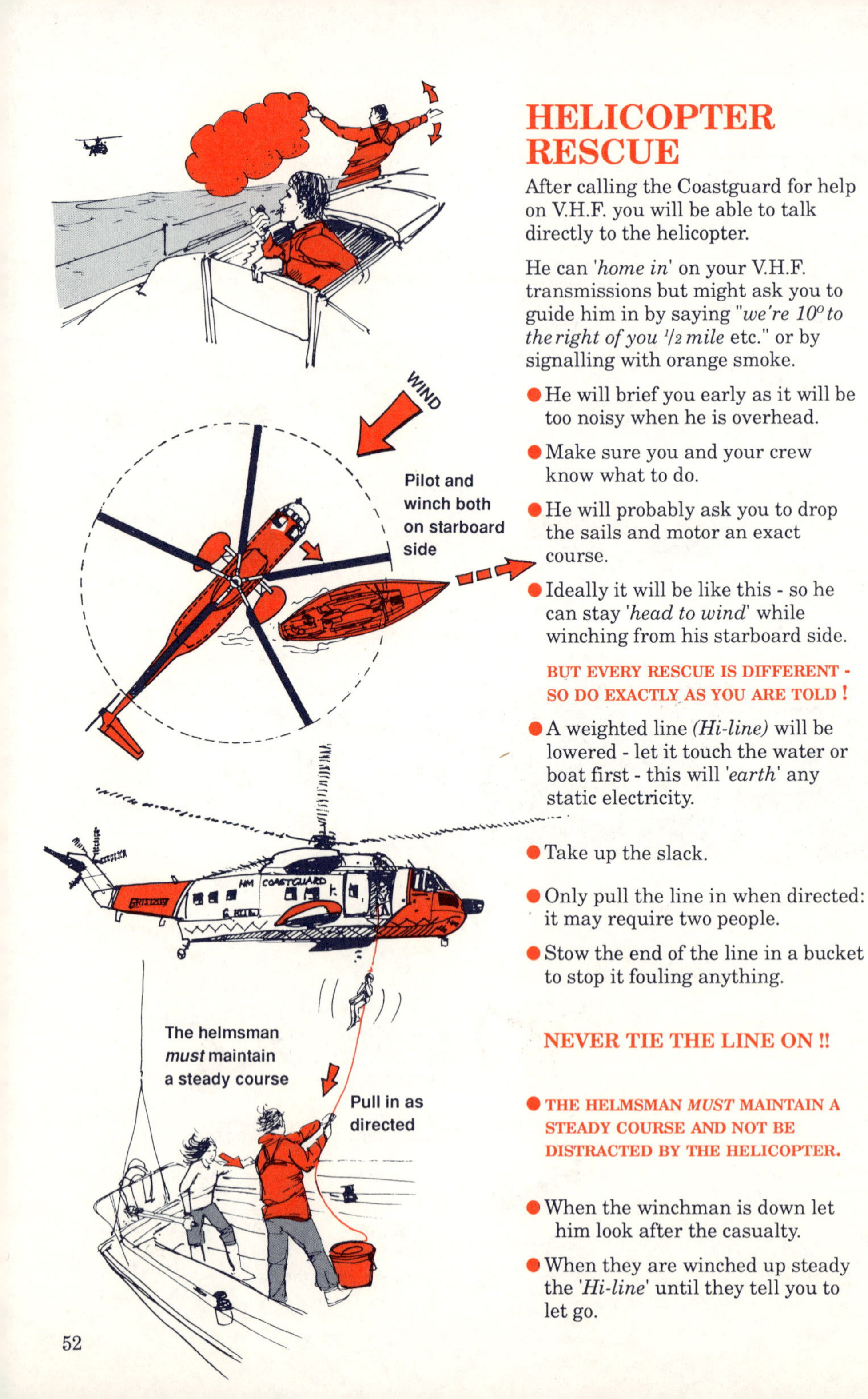

HELICOPTER RESCUE

After calling the Coastguard for help on V.H.F. you will be able to talk directly to the helicopter.

He can '*home in*' on your V.H.F. transmissions but might ask you to guide him in by saying "*we're 10° to the right of you ½ mile* etc." or by signalling with orange smoke.

- He will brief you early as it will be too noisy when he is overhead.
- Make sure you and your crew know what to do.
- He will probably ask you to drop the sails and motor an exact course.
- Ideally it will be like this - so he can stay '*head to wind*' while winching from his starboard side.

BUT EVERY RESCUE IS DIFFERENT - SO DO EXACTLY AS YOU ARE TOLD !

- A weighted line *(Hi-line)* will be lowered - let it touch the water or boat first - this will '*earth*' any static electricity.
- Take up the slack.
- Only pull the line in when directed: it may require two people.
- Stow the end of the line in a bucket to stop it fouling anything.

NEVER TIE THE LINE ON !!

- **THE HELMSMAN *MUST* MAINTAIN A STEADY COURSE AND NOT BE DISTRACTED BY THE HELICOPTER.**
- When the winchman is down let him look after the casualty.
- When they are winched up steady the '*Hi-line*' until they tell you to let go.

LIFERAFT

ONLY USE IT IF YOU ARE ABSOLUTELY SURE YOU ARE SINKING OR ON FIRE !

Stability and protection from the elements are largely a matter of size, so a yacht provides a greater potential for safety than a liferaft and it is also much easier to see.

REMEMBER - a great deal of water can be pumped out of a yacht by efficient bilge pumps.

Have the crew ready, wearing warm clothes, oilskins and life jackets. Also take emergency equipment such as flares, torch, water and emergency radio. Secure the '*static line*' and throw the raft over the '*lee*' side. It may be necessary to pull quite a long length (25ft) out of the raft to activate the bottle.

Try to keep dry boarding the raft. Put a strong man in first to help weaker members aboard. The raft will be most stable with its full complement of people on board. The '*static line*' is designed to pull away under load - it is not a painter to be used for holding a raft alongside for long periods.

When everyone is aboard, cut the line with the *special* knife which is positioned near the door. Get clear of the yacht and '*stream*' the '*drogue*'. The '*drogue*' is an integral part of the raft's stability system, it is not there only to reduce drift. If it is daylight, try to get the sea water batteries out of the water and save them until dark. Bale out the raft, and get into the 'space-blanket' survival bags (if supplied).

Position the crew around the raft in rough weather or have them huddle together to keep warm. Close the main canopy to save heat loss and make everyone take a seasick pill. Tie in the pump, as the raft will need to be 'topped-up' regularly. Pump up the double floor (if fitted) making sure you don't pump in any water. Post a look-out, ready with a flare, as ships will pass very quickly across your low horizon.

FIRST AID

We do no have enough space to cover this subject in full in this book.
For further information see the First Aid books in the current RYA catalogue. We also recommend attending a course so you can practice the techniques.
As skipper, you are responsible for the safety of the crew so you must curb dangerous over enthusiasm and order people to use safety gear - be it a safety-harness or a sun-hat.

PREVENTION IS BETTER THAN CURE.

Ask everyone if they have a medical problem (*such as diabetes or epilepsy etc.*) and find out what to do if anything goes wrong. (*Ask them as they are usually the experts.*)

SEA SICKNESS

This can spoil the day for everyone - so make sure potential sufferers take a tablet. (*It's not a bad idea to take one yourself as a good example !*) Often this simple act allays people's fears and they find their '*sea legs*' very quickly.
If you notice someone looking quiet and '*green*' give them something to do to take their mind off it. Steering is ideal ! Also don't let the crew eat and drink too much the night before sailing.

BLEEDING

'A little blood goes a long way - and looks frightening !'
Quickly find the wound and apply pressure - when it's cleaned up you'll probably only find a small cut, especially if it's on the head.

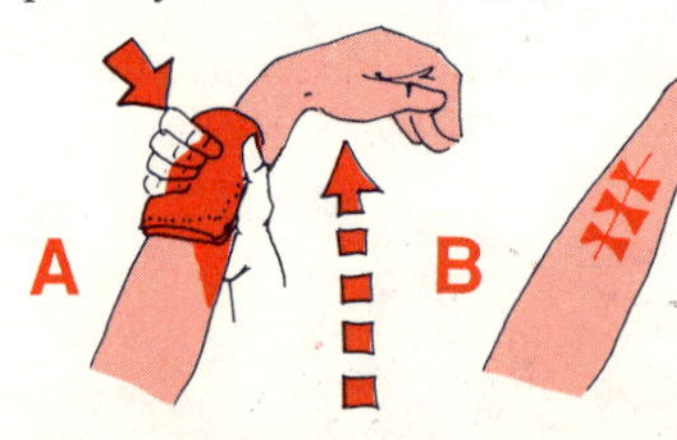

C D

A. FIRM PRESSURE STOPS ALMOST ANY BLEEDING
(providing there is nothing in the wound).
1. Press hard on the wound edges for up to 15 mins with a clean pad (or pinch skin together with your fingers for 5 mins).
2. If blood soaks through, leave in place and add another pad.
3. For arm or leg, raise it if possible to slow the blood flow.

B. A deep wound can be '*pulled together*' with butterfly plasters (or trimmed ordinary plasters).

C. If something is piercing the skin apply pressure around it. If it is a '*foreign body*' don't pull it out, as it could be acting as a plug. Make up pads around the object so the main pad won't press on the item directly. (If it protudes too far bandage around it.)

D. Always bandage up the limb over the pad. Finish it off with safety pins, tape or as here by splitting and tying the two ends in a knot.

CHECK THE BANDAGE ISN'T TOO TIGHT AND RESTRICTING BLOOD FLOW

THE KISS OF LIFE

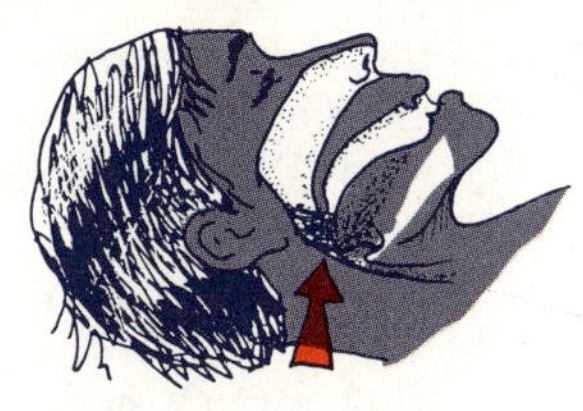

1. CLEAR THE AIRWAY
The airway may be blocked with vomit. Turn the head and scoop out with fingers.

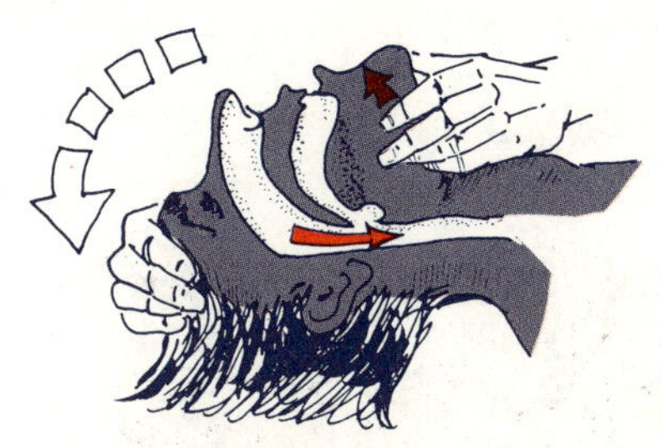

2. Lift the jaw and tip the head back.
This will raise the tongue and clear the airway. CHILDREN UNDER TWO: don't tip head back so far.

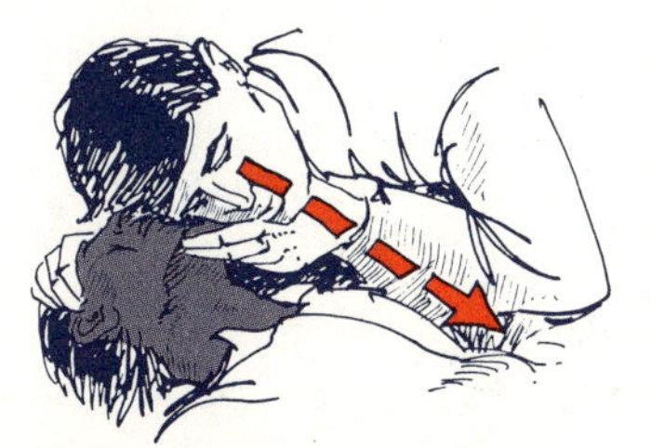

3. CHECK FOR SIGNS OF LIFE
Keep the airway open and listen for breathing - look to see if the chest is moving.
This is sometimes all that is needed

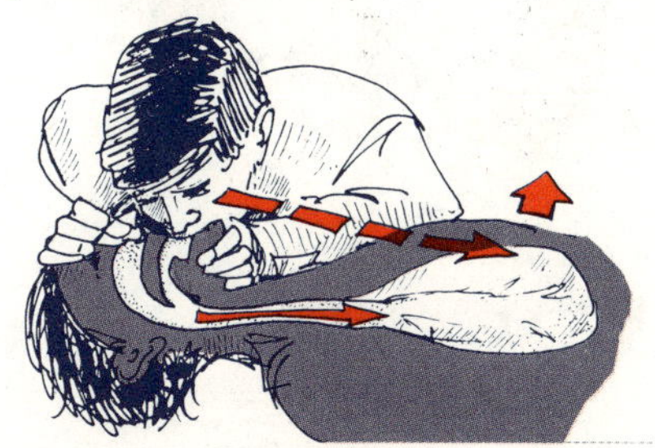

4. If they are not breathing -
START RESUSCITATION. Keep the head back, take a deep breath, pinch their nose and blow into the mouth. Check that the chest rises.

ALWAYS GIVE THE FIRST TWO INFLATIONS AS SOON AS POSSIBLE
DO NOT SPEND TIME LOOKING FOR HIDDEN OBSTRUCTIONS.

5. Remove your mouth, well away from the casualty's, and watch their chest fall.

6. Take a deep breath and repeat.

7. Continue at normal adult breathing rate until natural breathing is restored or until medical help arrives.

CHILDREN: blow gently at child's normal breathing rate.

Unfortunately vomiting nearly always occurs so many people carry one of the (one way valve) plastic barrier devices on board.

RECOVERY POSITION

ARM AND KNEE STRAIGHT

JAW FORWARD to maintain clear airway

ARM AND KNEE BENT

When they are breathing normally place in the 'recovery position'.
Keep warm and dry and secure them against the rolling of the vessel.
Don't leave them alone - keep checking they are O.K. and seek medical help.

YOU CAN GET MEDICAL ADVICE OVER THE RADIO BY CALLING ANY BRITISH COASTAL RADIO STATION USING THE PREFIX "**PAN, PAN, MEDICO**" - tell them which channels you have and they will link you to a doctor.

LIFEBOAT RESCUE

- Lifeboats over 10m can 'home in' on your normal VHF radio transmissions or EPIRB (if activated) - so keep calling at intervals even if you are not receiving.
- Always get the crew to prepare to abandon ship, while waiting, in case things become worse.
- Wear life-jackets, warm clothes and only take **small** valuables.
- The lifeboat is primarily for saving life but the cox'n may decide to save your boat as well. Prepare to be towed.

Bridle to spread load

get ALL lines in

If you are not sure how strong your cleats are - try to spread the load over several fittings with a '*bridle*' like this lead back to the sheet winches.

Use a double line for strength if possible.

PULL IN ALL THE LINES WHICH MIGHT FOUL THEIR PROP.

- If the cox'n decides to tow you, he might put a man on board to organize everything or they might throw you a '*heaving line*' - use this to pull in the tow rope.
- Secure the tow line to the '*bridle*'.
- If they can't get close, they might fire a thin '*gun-line*' - use this to haul in the '*heaving line*' THEN pull in the heavy tow line.

REMEMBER - THE LIFEBOAT IS THERE TO SAVE LIFE NOT ACT AS A TUG - SO DO EXACTLY AS THEY SAY - AND PLEASE DON'T FORGET TO THANK THEM !

TOWING

Arrange any fee before the tow starts.

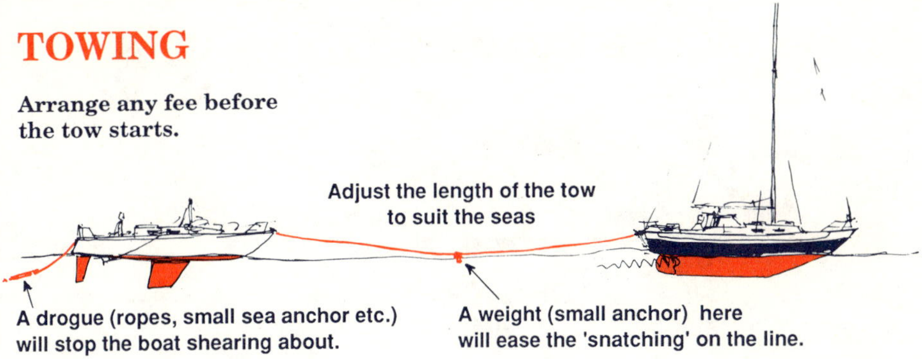

Adjust the length of the tow to suit the seas

A drogue (ropes, small sea anchor etc.) will stop the boat shearing about.

A weight (small anchor) here will ease the 'snatching' on the line.

Most yachts are not designed for towing so again you'll probably have to spread the load.

Here a' *bridle*' spreads the load and makes a more central pull.

The lines can be eased back if the '*anti-chafe*' protection around the ropes stars to wear.

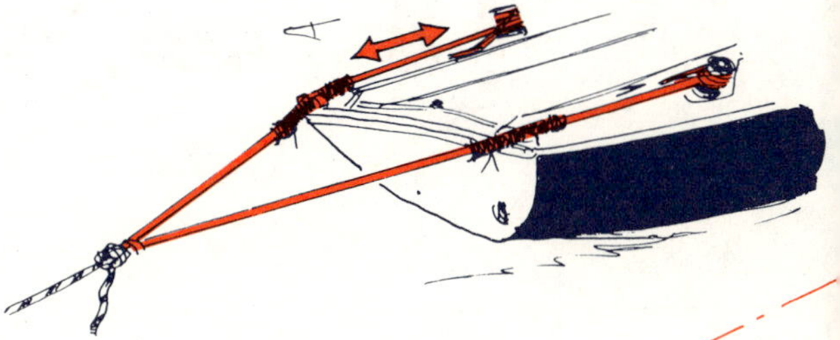

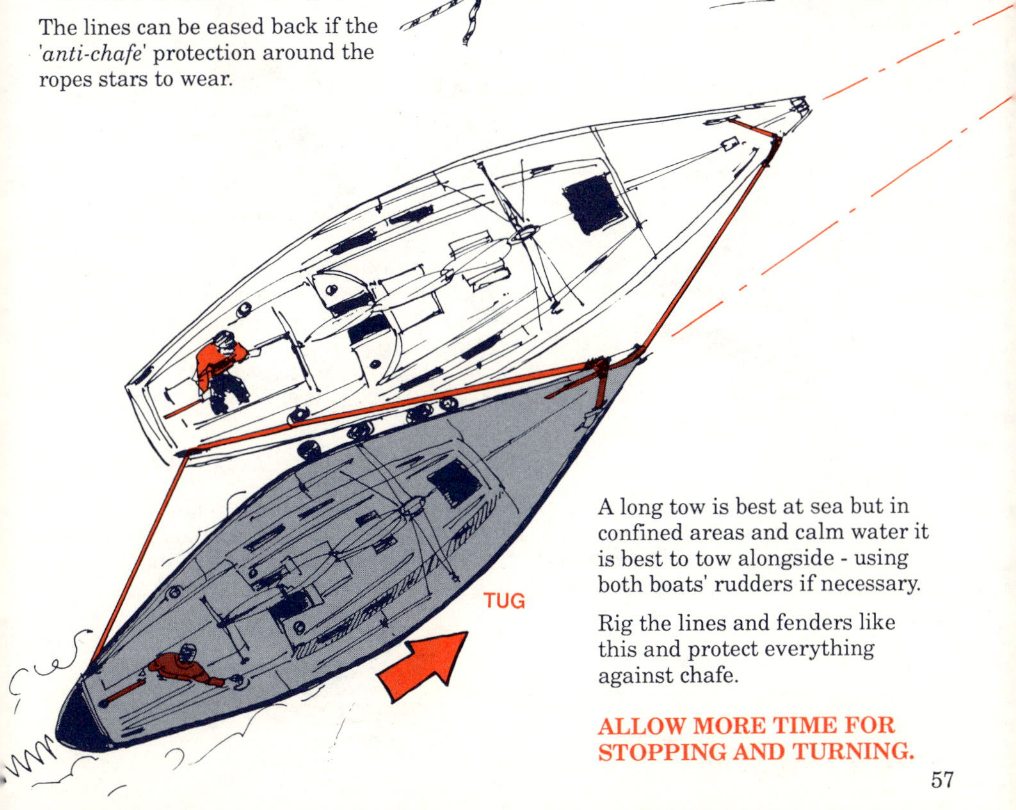

TUG

A long tow is best at sea but in confined areas and calm water it is best to tow alongside - using both boats' rudders if necessary.

Rig the lines and fenders like this and protect everything against chafe.

ALLOW MORE TIME FOR STOPPING AND TURNING.

RULES OF THE ROAD

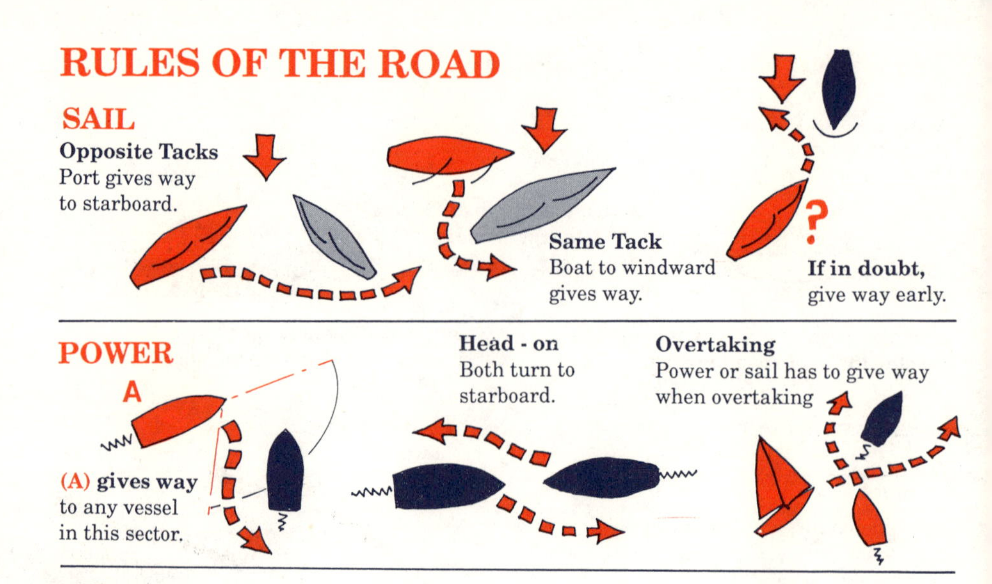

REAL LIFE

B

A

Don't assume that everyone knows the '*Rules of the Road*' - these two should give way BUT: **(A)** probably hasn't seen you and **(B)** might be racing and doesn't want you to hold him up. It might be courteous to make an early tack to avoid becoming the stand on vessel.

ALWAYS KEEP A GOOD LOOKOUT ...

Here, in what appears to us, is a large expanse of empty water is ... ...(A) a small fishing boat masked by our headsail and (B) coming up fast astern a large ship navigating in, what is to him, a narrow channel.

B

A

ARE WE GOING TO COLLIDE ?

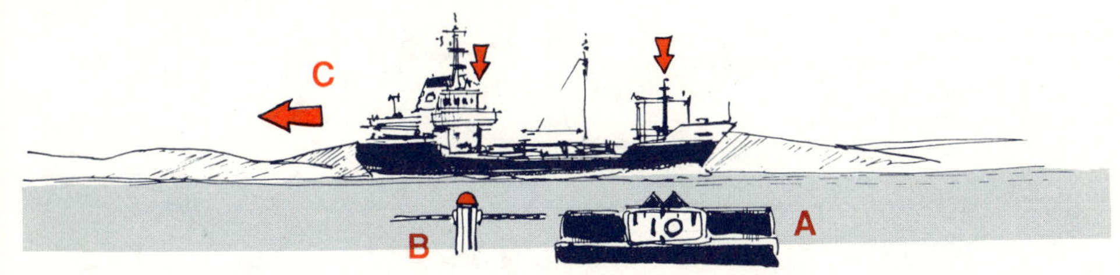

If a vessel maintains the same bearing to you, there will be a collision.

CHECK: **A.** The relative bearing, with a hand bearing compass.

B. If you are on a steady course line him up with a stanchion.

C. Does the background move from behind him ?

It is very difficult to judge the course and speed of ships in 'murky' weather - so be very careful of the 2nd and 3rd ones when trying to cross a line of shipping !

IF YOU MISJUDGE IT AND GET TOO CLOSE ...

... NEVER TURN TOWARDS THE SHIP
Always make a **definite** change of course **early** to avoid confusion.

A

B

(A) He might be turning to pass behind you **ALWAYS TURN AWAY** from him giving him a chance to swing back.**(B)**

LOOK OUT FOR THINGS LIKE ...

A. Tugs with their tow and line lost against the background in the haze.

B. Fishing vessels with gear trailing a long way astern.

C. Dredgers which are moored to several buoys fixed around them.
AND anything else that looks strange - give it a wide berth.

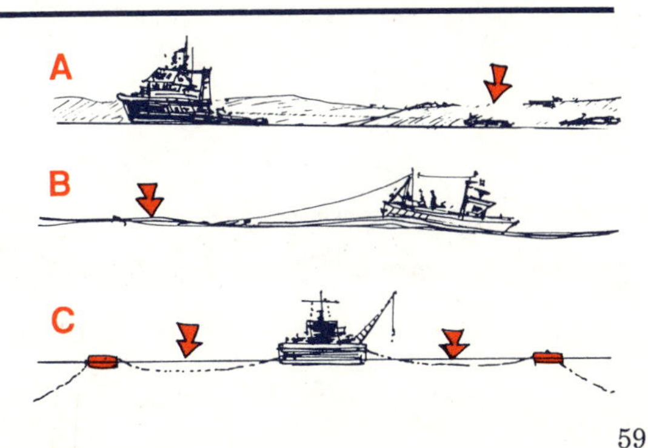

EASY MISTAKES TO MAKE

Although you have the latest chart you still have to proceed with caution because ...
... sandbanks can move, especially after a period of strong weather.
... channel edges can silt up particularly on the inside of bends where the flow is less and small navigation marks sometimes don't get moved to the new position.

THE CHART AND WHAT YOU SEE

The channel markers can often seem very clear on the chart ...

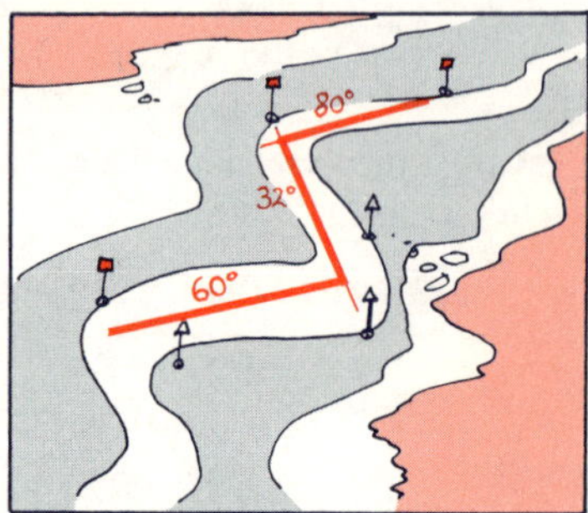

... but when you get there they can be obscured by other boats - it helps to draw bearing lines on the chart so you know where to look for the next mark.

SEEING THE NEXT MARK

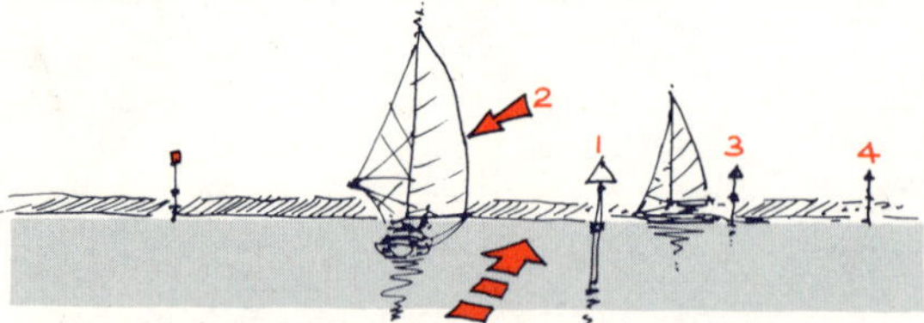

Here it looks as if we can just follow the starboard marks in - but '*look at the chart*', No2 marks a '*dog leg*' but it's hidden by the boat in front. It is too easy to go from No1 to No3 thinking it is the next mark.

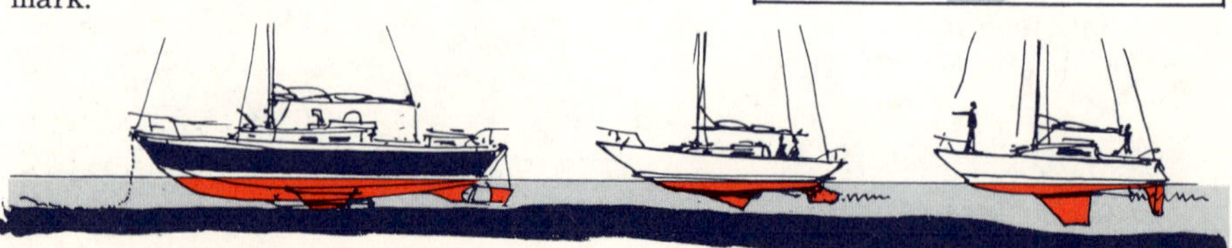

DON'T BLINDLY FOLLOW OTHERS ...

... assuming just because they are your size or bigger there'll be enough water for you. They might want to dry out for a scrub or have lifting keels !

WHERE IS THE DEEP WATER ?

Normally moorings are laid in deep water (but not always) near the edge of the channel ...

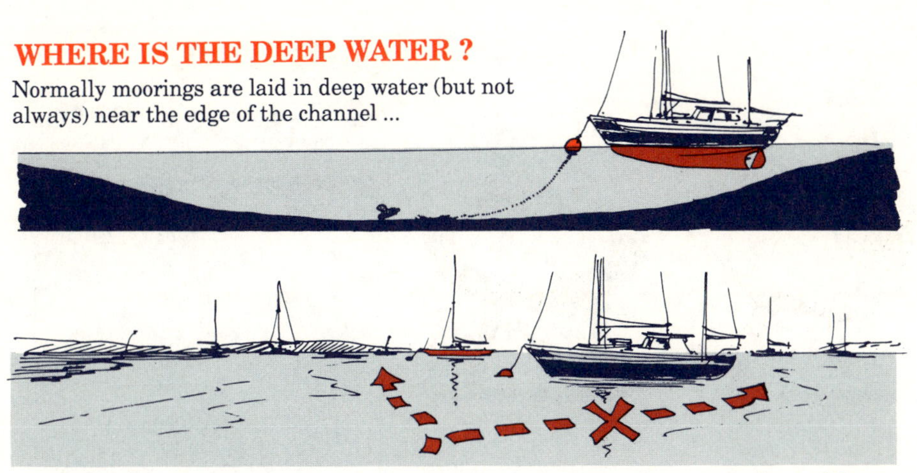

... so if the boats are floating and are *'wind rode'* it would be safer to go in front of them rather than behind them !

Here in what seems to be a vast expanse of water it might be prudent to stick close to the row of moorings to avoid the shallows.

TACKING UP NARROW CHANNELS

Best done on a flood tide.
Use your working jib for easy tacking and good visibility.

REMEMBER: at low water buoys can drift off giving a misleading impression of the width of the channel.
Don't leave the tack too late because channel edges move and you'll draw more water as the boat comes upright when you go about. Use your echo sounder

YOU'LL DRAW MORE WATER WHEN YOU GO ABOUT. DON'T LEAVE IT TOO LATE !

BUOY DRIFTED OFF AT LOW WATER

As skipper you can't give up navigating just because you are in harbour - you should have a mental picture of where the channel is - or if it's too complicated, keep a notebook in the cockpit. Only bring the chart on deck in fine weather.

DON'T JUST FOLLOW THE OTHER GUY - HE MIGHT BE LOST TOO !

AGROUND !

● **You need to act quickly if the tide is ebbing**

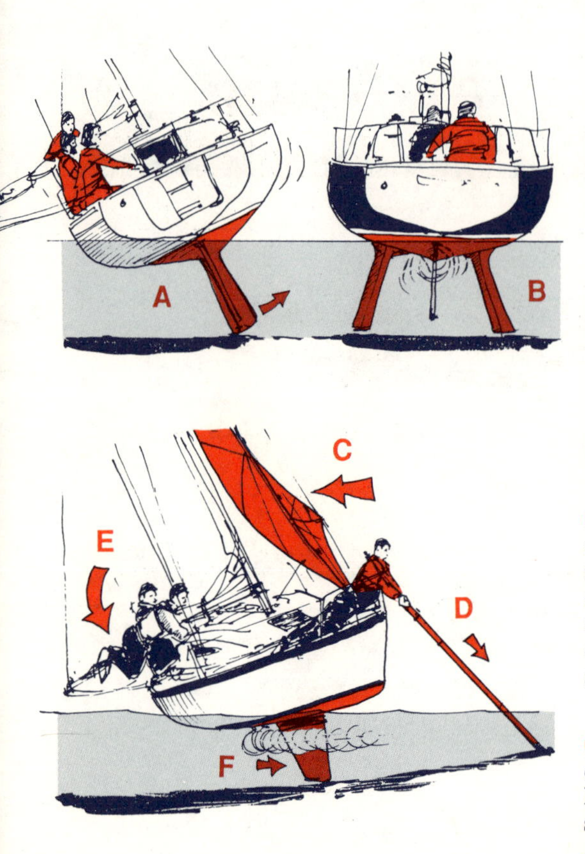

● If you sail on to a '*weather*' shore - sometimes you can gybe quickly and twist her off or back the headsail and free the main to bring the bow round. On a '*lee*' shore, it is more difficult, so you'll need to drop the sails and motor.

● If you get stuck, a fin keeler **(A)** can be '*heeled*' to reduce draught but keep a twin keeler **(B)** upright where she draws least.

● A short keel can be floated off by:

(C) *backing the headsail*

(D) *pushing the bow round*

(E) *heeling to reduce draught*

(F) *powering in reverse*

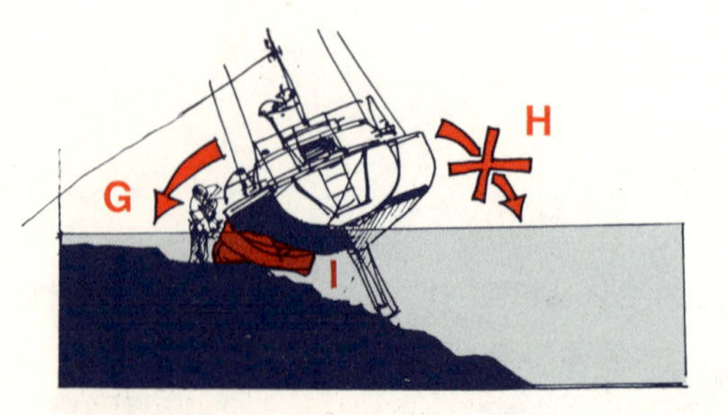

● If the tide is dropping fast and you can't get her off, heel her so she lays uphill **(G)** **not** downhill **(H)**. Protect the hull from rocks with mattresses etc **(I)** and maybe attach the dinghy to that side to help her lift again when the water returns.

● A VHF radio call to the coastguard would be a wise precaution.

LAYING OUT A KEDGE

● Make sure the kedge anchor is big enough - if not use the '*bower*'.

● Always put the anchor in the dinghy first and flake the cable in after it.

The cable must be free to run **from the dinghy** as you row away. (Some people add 20ft or so of extra light line to allow the dinghy to go that bit further and use this 'extra' bit to haul in the slack when the anchor is down.)

● Row well **uptide** if the current is strong - when all the cable is out and you're in the right position lower the anchor. (This is often easier if there are two in the dinghy.)

● Haul in the cable from the yacht.

TAKING COMMAND

A GOOD SKIPPER	A BAD SKIPPER
Plans manouevres in advance considering wind and tide then briefs the crew.	Disregards wind and tide, doesn't inform the crew, then shouts at them when things go wrong.
Marks up the tidal stream atlas before leaving and knows how to use it.	Ignores tidal streams resulting in slow inaccurate navigation.
Checks high and low waters and makes port entries with a clear idea of the state of the tide.	Runs aground when entering harbour or grounds overnight at anchor.
Considers what to do if a crew member falls overboard.	Loses crew.
Listens to weather forecasts and plans accordingly.	Gets 'caught out' in adverse weather.
Sets the sails efficiently.	Pulls in the sails and leaves them there.
Keeps the yacht tidy below and cleans up spills.	Throws everything in a heap and treads spilt soup all over the boat.
Understands basic engine maintenance.	Never opens the engine box.
Notices chafe and other problems on deck.	Waits until equipment breaks before replacing it.
Pre-plans meals and ensures sufficient food and drink on board.	Hopes to buy fish and chips on arrival.
Knows how to use the emergency equipment.	Waits until a crisis before finding out how to use the emergency equipment.
Runs a happy ship and enjoys it.	Runs a miserable ship and only enjoys talking about it afterwards.